BUILDING
Successful Relationships

Successful Relationships

keys
to
winning
and
keeping
the
hearts
of
others

by

Michael Fletcher

ISBN 1-58502-032-X

Published by:
Advancethekingdom.com
5117 Cliffdale Road
Fayetteville, N.C. 28314
910-867-9151

Printed in the United States of America

Cover & interior by idesignetc. idesignetc@adelphia.net

1 2 3 4 5 6 7 8 9 0 / 08 07 06 05 04

Table of Contents

Introduction

You picked this book up for a reason. Something about winning or keeping the heart of another person attracted your attention. Perhaps you desire to strengthen an already great marriage or maybe mend a damaged one. Perhaps you are grieving the loss of a broken friendship or pining over the departure of a wayward child. You might be looking for ways to strengthen or expand your client base. Maybe you are just searching for a friend. Whatever your goal or desire is, if it comes to establishing new relationships in the future, fixing broken ones from the past, or making your present relationships stronger, you have come to the right place. When you finish this book, you will have the tools you need to do all three! The healthy relationships you have will be stronger. You will be on a new path to restore the broken ones. And, you will know how to establish new healthy relationships that really last!

All of life is about relationships

Every person coming into the world gets here through a family. Now, that family may be broken before the person is born, but it took a family, or a family of sorts, to produce a child. Before that child knows anything about life, he is already wrapped up in relationships. Everything about those relationships will affect his life in potentially dramatic ways. Whether the father is present and in love with the child's mother, or is absent and estranged from the mother will have a bearing on the course of the child's life. If the doctors and nurses who participate in his birth are experiencing stress from personal relationships that are falling apart, his quality of care may be affected.

This little fellow has no control over these circumstances, and thus no control over these relationships. But as he grows, he gains more control over the relationships that surround his life. And relationships are everywhere! Relationships with parents, grandparents, friends, teachers, and classmates govern his early childhood. Counselors, girlfriends (watch out!), coaches, teammates, enemies, rivals, and professors shape his youth. Relationships with his spouse, children (every child is different!), in-laws, bosses, clients, business contacts, old friends, new friends, used-to-be friends—all these fill and influence his life. Relationships are everywhere, because all of life is about relationships. If anyone is going to be successful in life, they are going to have to be successful in relationships!

The success or failure of our relationships directly affects the quality of life we enjoy

All my life I have heard people speak of success in terms of money in the bank. The thought is that the greater the bank balance, the higher the quality of life a person enjoys; but, I have learned in over twenty years of ministry to people, that this is one of life's great deceptions.

Onc of the most successful physicians in our city was in my office. As he waited patiently for me in the waiting room of our office suite (what goes around comes around!), numbers of people recognized him as a well respected member of the medical community. To look at him from the outside, he had it all together. Not that we talked about it or even that he volunteered the information, but to look at his bank account one would be very impressed. He was known to be among the more financially successful doctors in our community. But inside he was a broken and desperate mess! His marriage was secretly, but soon-to-be not so secretly, falling apart. He opened up to a friend who sent him to me. And there he was, slowly decomposing in front

> Relationships are everywhere, because all of life is about relationships. If anyone is going to be successful in life, they are going to have to be successful in relationships!

of me as he shared his tragic story. He could have used the relational truths contained in this book ten years ago. In all seven areas that I will cover, he had fallen short and his marriage was an apt portrayal of the results.

Interestingly, outside in the waiting area sat a number of people waiting for appointments with members of my staff. None of them had the kind of investment account this doctor had. None of them drove the kind of car he drove. But all of them were infinitely happier in their relationships than he. Now, who had enjoyed the better quality of life?

Am I saying that you can't have money and happiness? No way! I know plenty of wealthy people who enjoy life tremendously. All I am saying is that money does not determine your quality of life—relationships do! The most important things in life are not defined in terms of dollars and cents, but in terms of people. The people in our life or the lack there of, powerfully impact our happiness and in large measure determine our quality of life.

> **Money does not determine your quality of life—relationships do! The most important things in life are not defined in terms of dollars and cents, but in terms of people.**

You did not need to read this to know that. You have already experienced the power and the pain of this truth in your own life. There have been times when all of the troubles of this life seemed to fade away because of that "special someone." You looked across the room and there he was. All of a sudden you forgot everything else because you knew he was "the one." Or your teenage daughter stepped into your room just before heading off to bed to tell you how much she appreciated all you do for her and what a great mother you have been. You smiled and thanked her as she left your room, but you couldn't sleep because of the joy and the realization that "it really is all worth it!"

There have also been the times when you saw your "best friend" out on the town with another friend for the third time in a row. You remember the sorrow of realizing that they may be your best friend, but you aren't their best friend. Not only was it a painful realization, but you felt so foolish as well! Perhaps you woke up one morning and finally faced the fact that you no longer really knew the person whose head was on the pillow beside you. As you lay there in painful silence, you can't remember when the downward slide began or how it all started, but you realize you are at the bottom, and the "spark" is totally gone.

Every one of us has stories of success and failure in relationships. The tragedy is that most of us do not know what made for that success or failure. Why do some relationships thrive while others do not? Is there a rhyme or a reason to the relationship game? Yes, I believe there is! I believe there is one key universal truth with seven applications that determines the future of every relationship. I know that is a bold statement, but read on and see if the ideas contained here don't make sense. The truth is that a closer examination of the successes and failures you have already had will reveal the same thing. I did not just wake up with this idea. First, these ideas came to light through my study of the Scriptures, God's handbook for life. Second, I have watched how these truths worked in dealing with thousands of people over the years.

So why did you pick up this book?

What was it about winning or keeping the heart of another that caught your eye? Are you interested in making new friends? Are you trying to bolster a struggling marriage? Are you concerned about your connection to your sons and daughters? Are you alone and looking for companionship? Perhaps you are looking for a boost in your business relationships to help put you "over the edge" of financial success. Get ready! The adventure is about to begin. But let me warn you, at some point you are going to say, "No way, this is too easy!" But give these ideas a try and you will see that they really do work.

Questions for your relational journey

1. All of life is about relationships. What different kinds of relational roles do you find yourself in (i.e. spouse, parent, employee, coach, friend, etc)?

2. The success or failure of these relationships directly affects the quality of life that we enjoy. How have you found that to be true in your own life?

3. What is your motivation for reading this book? What are you hoping to gain?

"One Profound Truth!"

Keep your heart with all diligence, for out of it spring the issues of life.

Proverbs 4:23 (NKJV)

The New International version of the bible translates the above verse as follows: *"Above all else, guard your heart, for it is the wellspring of life."* Either way, it is a simple but very profound verse. The truth contained here can impact and dramatically revolutionize your life. Here we are told three important things in just a few short words.

The heart, the center of life

First, we find out that at the center of life resides the heart. It is the "governing organ of the soul" according to Biblical theologians. The "heart" spoken of here is not the physical pump that runs our circulatory system, but the very center of our life. It is what makes us human. Jesus Himself said that everything that flows out of a person's mouth finds its origin in the heart[1]. Whatever this heart is, it is very important. But we already know that. Often when people experience joy they will say, "It thrilled my heart." When we are profoundly disappointed or sad we will sometimes say, "It broke my heart." When we take another in holy matrimony, we may say, "I give you my heart." When we fall in love unexpectedly we might say, "He stole my heart." When we really desire something we say, "I have my heart set on it." In many other ways, the human experience portrays through the common language of life that the heart is the most important part of a person.

Giving your heart away

Second, we are told to keep or guard our hearts. The reason is obvious—the heart is easily captured by other people. When that happens we put ourselves into another person's hands. That can be a wonderful thing! In fact, life can only truly be lived when our hearts are in the hands of others.

As soon as a new mother holds her little newborn for the first time, she instantly gives her heart away. The look on her face is worth more than money can buy. I know, I have seen it eight times, each time one of my children came into the world. My wife, Laura, in that moment was able to put all the pain of the hours that preceded aside, because something—someone— had captured her heart. Her face took on a new glow as she tenderly stroked the face of a tiny new Fletcher. Each time I had to fight back tears as I recognized a bond that was instant, permanent, and holy—something that existed only between the two of them. It happened because my wife gave her heart away, immediately and without reservation. I have also seen the afterglow of that look on the faces of countless other mothers

> Life can only truly be lived when our hearts are in the hands of others.

as I visited them in the hospital on the maternity floor. I saw that same look on the face of the wife of one of my staff members during a movie. They were unaware that, coming in after the previews, we snuck into a seat right behind them. During the show, in the middle of the action, I saw her turn and just look up at the face of her husband, totally oblivious to the movement on the screen. And there it was—that look—that look that said, "I have given my heart completely to you, and that decision has brought me into a place of security and joy. I am totally satisfied that I will belong to you and you only for the rest of my life." Yes, giving our hearts away is the key to happiness.

No one is safe from the "dangers" of love

But the admonition to "guard" is there for a reason. Giving our hearts to others also puts us in a position to experience pain. I have seen that pain on the faces of many people and have experienced it myself. When we give our heart to another, we give them a piece of ourselves—and not just any piece—the most important piece. That's why we are often hurt the most by those we love. It is that love that opens us up to them and them to us. The more open and vulnerable we become, the more we give our heart away, and the more potential for joy and intimacy as well as hurts and pain.

Theft of the heart

If that were the end of the story, life would be easy. We would simply make a careful study of potential friends and lovers and only give our hearts to the most trustworthy among them. Our experience tells us that life works differently. All of us have had folks worm their way into our hearts in ways we didn't expect. The story of many a romance begins with the tale of a persistent pursuer, who, at first resisted, continued to pursue. The tellers of the tale laugh as they reminisce about, "how I never thought," and "who would have known."

Proverbs 4:23 warns us to "guard" because our hearts are so easily subject to theft! C.S. Lewis said it best in *The Four Loves* when he said that only in heaven and hell would we be safe from the dangers of love; in heaven, because love is perfect and in hell because love is absent. Of what dangers did he speak? The dangers that come from the fact that in this life, we are always subject to the theft of our hearts. Once love has taken hold, the object of that love is in control. Things will change; plans change; our life changes. Well-thought-out decisions come into question all because of love.

My father said no more animals—emphatically and definitely. He was deaf to our cries and pleading. No more pets! All that ended when we brought that little kitten home. Dad started off with, "We can not keep that thing. Why did you bring this cat home!?" Moments later it became, "Only for tonight but after you clean it up, it has to go!" The next day it went to, "Now, I am not going to be responsible for taking care of that cat!" You know the drill, once he saw it and gave it a little time, the little furry bundle who could not speak our language was getting a portion of my father's income in vet bills and food!

Whoever has your heart has your life!

The most important idea contained here is that all of life springs forth from the heart. That is the key treasure of truth we are here to mine. The bottom line is this, whoever has your heart has your life. No more profound truth could be spoken about human relationships than that. In this truth is the key to present and future happiness and the explanation of past and present pain! If you only underline one thing in this book, underline this, whoever has your heart has your life!

Let me illustrate. Over the years I have had the unfortunate occasion to witness, far too many times, the transference of allegiance of children from their parents to their peers, often resulting in tragic consequences. When children are young they depend on their parents for almost everything. Sometimes as they grow, they undergo a shift from parent dependency to peer dependency. There is nothing wrong with children making friends. In fact, they will not be healthy without friends, but friends and peer dependency are two different things.

> If your only underline one thing in this book, underline this, whoever has your heart has your life!

How does this happen? It is simple. The parents lost the heart of their child. Some friend or group of friends has the heart of the child now and things begin to change. The values the son or daughter grew up with begin to be challenged. Next comes the establishment of new authorities. No more going to mom and dad for advice. The new friends are the consultants for life now. Fights between parent and child become more volatile and frequent.

The truth is that children of all ages can build strong vibrant friendships and still enjoy a healthy relationship with their parents. There is room in the heart for everyone. In the situation above, the parents lost the heart of their child and, consequently, the child went looking for a place to give it and found some willing takers in their friends. Does this have to happen? No way!

Another example of this truth is found in many struggling marriages. Allen knows something is wrong but he can't put his finger on it. Something is missing in his marriage. When he asks Allyson if everything is okay with her, her answers are vague. Suspicion grows and so do the rumors of an affair with Allen's best friend. Finally, one day in the heat of battle, he confronts her. Stunned, her mouth says nothing, but her face says it all. How did this happen? Weeks later Allen sits incredulously in the counselor's office. Allyson says it wasn't about sex, and the counselor agrees. She says it *became* sexual. What happened? Allen stopped nurturing her heart, and it was given to another. When Allen's best friend had her heart, he had her life, sex and all! Somewhere along the line Allen failed to recognize that he was losing Allyson's heart. He was completely unaware that she was beginning to give her heart to someone else. What could Allen have done differently?

Let me say it again. The reason we have to guard the heart is because whoever has the heart has the life. In every relationship you now enjoy, that is exactly what happened. You won the heart of another. With every friendship, you won their heart. With your spouse, you won his or her heart. As your aunt's favorite, you enjoyed a greater piece of her heart than the other nieces and nephews. The same holds true with your children. When a child is born, they experience "need love" toward their parents. They love their parents because their parents meet their needs. Over time, that love slowly matures. As mom and dad instinctively love and care for their child, that child's heart is freely given to them.

Keeping the Hearts of Others

The exciting thing is this—the things you do to *win* a person's heart are the very same things you do to *keep* it. The trouble is that once we win a person's heart, we often do not continue in the pattern we started. Often that is because *we do not know what we did* to win the person's heart in the first place! So, we "take life as it comes" and wonder why some of our relationships work and some do not. We look across the street in amazement and wonder what the neighbors did to have such great teenagers when ours do not want to have a thing to do with us. After a string of lost friendships or years of no friendships at all, we wonder if there is something wrong with us. It's not us. It is our application of this simple but profound truth; whoever has the heart has the life!

The Most Important Thing

The third important idea outlined in Proverbs 4:23 is that we should apply *diligence* to this pursuit; and not just diligence, *all diligence*. The other translation sited uses the words "above all else." In other words, "this is the most important thing!" Life is full of areas that require skill, but none are more important than relational skills. We need to become experts at winning and keeping the hearts of others. Our happiness depends on it, because our relationships depend on it.

So, let's get busy. There is no question that this is going to require time, and energy. Some of the ways we conduct ourselves in our relationships may have to change. Change is not easy, but change in this area of life will yield tremendous blessings and benefits.

From my experience, I have found that there are seven

powerful principles that we can use to gain and keep the hearts of others. Some or all of these principles were in operation when you first won another's heart. The continued application of them is key to your keeping that heart. The principles are as follows:

1. **Love**—Loving others without condition

2. **Faith**—Believing more for someone than they do for themselves

3. **Interest**—Placing value on what is important to others

4. **Availability**—Making room for others in crisis and in life

5. **Respect**—Establishing a person's worth

6. **Time**—The key to unlocking a heart

7. **Communication**—The lifeline to every relationship

Now, let's begin. In the following chapters, I will lay out each of these seven principles and show you how their application will change your life for the better.

Questions for your relational journey

1. The heart is easily captured by other people. Think of a time when another person unexpectedly won your heart.

2. Giving our heart away is a key to happiness. Why are people so reluctant to do that?

3. Who has your heart? How is it that they "have your life?"

4. Have you ever had a relationship fall apart? Look at the list of seven items at the end of this chapter. Which of these seven waned during the life of that relationship leading to its demise?

Notes

1. Matthew 10:34

chapter 2

Love
Loving others without condition

For God so loved the world that He gave His
one and only Son, that whoever believes in Him
shall not perish but have eternal life.

John 3:16

Rock and Roll icon Tina Turner belted out tunes for years on her way to musical stardom. Many became hits in terms of universal recognition, but in 1984, she released her most popular song, "What's love got to do with it?"[1] The chorus goes "What's love got to do with it? What's love, but a second hand emotion?" In the mid 90's, a movie was made about Ms. Turner's life with this song serving as the theme. To answer her question "what's love go to do with it?"...everything! Later in the song she sings, "Who needs a heart when a heart can be broken?" We are all familiar with Tina Turner's story of surviving an abusive marriage. Her experience of love is not one any of us would want to live out in our personal relationships. Many of us have already seen the kind of pain portrayed in this song and have had our fill. Our goal is to live a life full of happy and healthy life long relationships.

We need to decide on our definition of love

If love is only an emotion, then maybe Tina was right. Maybe we shouldn't put too much stock in the idea, since we all know that emotions can change in an instant. We would be fools to put our hearts into the hands of those driven solely by emotion. Love based on emotions is bound to last only as long as that emotion. What a frightful thought!

Many of us have made that fateful mistake. We entered into a relationship based on how we felt at the time. Both parties started out at the same relative level of emotion, but eventually one started to grow emotionally colder. That's when the trouble started. At first we tried to hold on to what we felt was fading away. Then, perhaps we tried the "I too can play it cool" tactic, only to find out that the other person was glad we were starting to allow for a little distance in our relationship. It was then that the real pain started to set in, as our once close relationship was reduced to a level that was more distant than when it began.

Thankfully, love is not just an emotion. Love produces emotions. We would be foolish to confuse the emotional product of love for love itself. Many people seek the emotion, not realizing that, in so doing, they are sowing the seeds of destruction into the foundation of their relationship. They wind up building on the wrong thing—on the emotion of love, and not on the sure foundation that true love provides.

When we focus on the emotional side of love, we make our goal to keep the emotion going. We like it. It makes us feel good. Very quickly we become dependent on that emotion. It is like a drug. When that emotion is flowing through our veins, we have new perspective. Old troubles seem manageable. New problems look more like opportunities, since "together we can lick anything." We are high on life, because we are high on the emotion of love. Unless we have built something other than this potentially fleeting emotion into the foundation of our relationship, we will have nothing upon which to land when the high is over.

I have been happily married to the same special woman for over 25 years. Not only do I love her, but I am *in love* with her. I am in no way against the emotion of love; I love the byproduct of true love. Life would be so boring without it. All I am saying is that the emotion of love is not all that love is about. We have to be careful to keep the horse in front of the cart. True love produces the emotion of love, but true love lasts even when the emotion fades away.

Infatuation

"I have loved him from the first day I saw him in class!" "I loved my third grade teacher!" "I loved Paul McCartney!" This kind of "love" is infatuation. Basically, infatuation is being in love with the idea of being in love. For those who have fallen into it, infatuation looks a lot like love, and discerning the difference from the inside can be difficult. But the two are miles apart.

> Infatuation is about me and what I am getting from this relationship, so it is inherently selfish.

Infatuation has, as its focus, how another makes you feel and the benefit you receive from being with them. A high school girl does not see herself as just a high school girl when she is on the arm of a college boy. A guy jumps way up on the ladder of popularity when the head cheerleader accepts his invitation to the prom. He steps up even higher if he can be seen with her the next day or so, and even higher if he gets her to wear his ring. In the same way, the secretarial pool is buzzing when it is discovered that, the flowers on the desk of one of their own, are from the new single Junior Exec down the hall.

In the end, infatuation is about me and what I am getting from this relationship, so it is inherently selfish. Much like building a relationship on the emotion of love, infatuation is flawed from the start and cannot be considered true love.

Lust

"If you loved me you would ..." has been the opening line to many a disaster. How many young adults have given up what they planned to keep until marriage, in response to this idea? Love and lust are totally different. In fact they are opposites. But people, led by the emotion of the moment, confuse hormones with love and fall into the trap. Relationships built on lust never last. Lust, being inherently self-centered, is never satisfied and constantly seeks new levels of excitement. As soon as that which is provided by a person becomes routine, the one driven by lust will seek out more.

Paul and Cindy loved each other deeply, or so she thought. He couldn't keep his hands off her. He'd never known anyone like her. "Since we're going to get married anyway, don't you think that we can ... and how about trying ...?" The sex was great! They couldn't wait to get married. It can only get better, right? Wrong! Once they were married, the guilt settled in on her. The excitement of having to sneak around was gone, and it became old hat for him. Finally, Paul found others with whom he could satisfy his misplaced passion. He was sneaking again. It was forbidden, and he was excited once more. One adulterous relationship led to another, and eventually Cindy found out.

Today they are divorced. You can not build lasting relationships on lust, because lust can never really be satisfied.

Conditional "need love"

Many people confuse "need love" with true love as well. Need love is the kind of love that everyone has for those providing their primary care in the early stages of life. A baby loves her mother because her mother feeds and cares for her. That process of nurturing breeds an atmosphere of security where trust and dependency is developed. The baby feels safe. All her needs are being met. Over time, that love matures as the child matures, and mom is loved as much for who she is as for what she provides.

Unfortunately, many people try to build lasting relationships on this kind of love with tragic results. "I meet your needs and you meet mine." That sounds great, but what happens if I stop meeting your needs? Will you still love me? Or do you love me because I meet your needs? Your love for me, then, is conditioned upon what I do for you. If I ever stop meeting your needs, you will stop loving me, and our relationship will be over. So many relationships are built just this way, even in families. Often parents give or withhold love based on the performance of their child. If the child obeys, then the love flows freely. If the child rebels, then the love is withheld. Love should never be the reward for good behavior. Love should be a gift a child receives from a parent regardless of their behavior. When parents relate to their children based on their behavior, they communicate to their children that love is conditional and must be earned.

True love centers on unconditional giving

The verse listed at the outset of this chapter is probably the most quoted verse from the Bible, because it captures the essence of the Christian faith. But it captures more than that. It includes the best definition of the true character of love I have ever found:

"For God so loved . . . that He gave . . ." [2]

True love always centers on giving without regard to what we get in return. This is how God loved us, and this is how we are to love others as well.

The real trouble with love as an emotion, or infatuation, or need love, or lust, is that they all share the same tragic flaw—each one centers on what we *receive* from a relationship. Each, therefore, seeks to build our relationships on the shifting ground of self, and has as its goal, to see what we can get from these relationships. Disappointed when our goals and needs go unmet, we get angry and withdraw our love in return.

> True love always centers on giving without regard to what we get in return.

There is an epidemic of confusion as to the true definition of love in the world today. Most of our past relationships have trained us to "look out for number one." If a relationship doesn't meet our needs, we dump it and move on. Most people hold as a sacred truth that "there is no free lunch." We are trained from our youth that everyone is out for something, and everything comes with conditions lodged deep in the fine print.

The church should model Christ's love

The church universal has done a pretty poor job of communicating to the world the true message of the Christian faith. We have allowed them to believe that God requires adherence to a certain set of laws before they can find His love and acceptance. The truth is that God gave His Son for us with no strings attached so that none would perish. Jesus took our penalty and removed the barrier between man and God. The message of Christianity is not rules and regulations but love without condition.

Our church has attempted to help undo this misconception by engaging in service projects in our community designed to communicate that God loves people with no strings attached. We wash cars at no charge and refuse donations in return. We give away thousands of cold drinks on hot days all over the city, refusing payment. We have washed toilets in area businesses and given away hot dogs and drinks at local festivals. We never invite folks to visit or join our church. We never ask or receive any payment. When people ask why we would do such a thing, we simply respond, "We just wanted to show you that God loves you in a practical way!" Usually they shake their heads and ask, "What is the catch? What is your angle?" To which we respond, "We don't have an angle, just love, nothing added, nothing required." Some folks can't take it; it doesn't compute in the modern cynical mind. They demand that we take payment. The epidemic of confusion, as to the true definition of love, is widespread!

> The message of Christianity is not rules and regulations but love without condition.

True love gives

Let me make this very clear. True love is not oriented toward what we can get out of a relationship but what we can give. True love says, "I have found in you a person I choose to love, and I am determined to demonstrate that love to you by meeting your needs, whether you meet mine or not. I give myself to you and expect nothing in return." That is true love. When we demand our love to be returned or expect that our needs be met, we clearly communicate that our love is conditional.

Sometimes parents will respond to a rebellious child with increasing expectations—that the love they have so freely given over the years be returned through, at least, respect from their son or daughter. That increased demand is often met by increased rebellion and the parents wonder why. The love they have freely given is now being redefined as conditional in the heart and mind of their child. The teen now thinks, "You say you love me, but you only love me so I will respect you. Fine, I'll respect you, but don't expect me to love you in return. And when I leave your home, don't look for any respect either!" Parents sometimes forget that the most powerful thing they could do is love their child despite the rebellion. Continue to touch the teen and invite him into your life. Reach for him emotionally and never give up on him, even in the midst of the storm. The Bible says it is the goodness of God that leads us to repentance[3]. It is so disarming to have done something wrong, but to be loved in the midst of it anyway.

True love includes discipline

I am not saying that anything goes in every relationship. Every relationship has its parameters, and there is a time to be tough in relationships. But even when we are tough, we need to coat everything, even discipline, with love. In fact, true love includes discipline, and true discipline, if properly administered, is loving. Love is sometimes firm and unbending. Love sometimes holds up a standard that is unpopular. Love always does what is best for another, even when they do not understand or appreciate it. Certainly, children require clear and definite direction, and shaping them in the early years requires strong and steady discipline; but our actions toward them must always be motivated and couched in an attitude of love.

People are drawn to those who truly love them

Albert's father died when he was very young, and his single mother did the very best she could to raise him, but times were tough and so was he. Albert was supposedly a part of the youth group I led, but he hardly ever came; and when he did, he figured it was his part-time job to be aloof but disruptive. He was "cool." When he came, I reached out to him. Although he did his best to be unlovable, I determined to love him. One evening, while at home with his mother, he became belligerent to the point of being violent. His single mother feared for the safety of the other children and sent them out of the house. Not knowing what else to do, she called me. By the time I got there, Albert was in a rage. My presence only made things worse—his mother had called in "the authorities!" "F... God! F... the church! F... you!" he said over and over. He threw iced tea at me along with other items in the house. I stood there soaking wet and told Albert in no uncertain terms, "I don't care what you say about God, the church, or me. I love you and will continue to love you no matter what you do or where you go. And if you run from here, I'll just pray that God will raise someone up to love you in the very same way." Albert did run and to my knowledge is still running but for years he called me (even once from prison) to see how things were going and to share a piece of his life. Why? Because of the power of unconditional love! People are drawn to those who love them without expecting anything in return. It creates a trust. Not to mention the fact that you are meeting one of life's most basic needs. People crave love. They are irresistibly drawn to those who provide it.

True love can change a community

Carolynne is a lady who, most would say, is average in many ways. She is a middle class woman who lives in a middle class house and enjoys the same middle class lifestyle as do others in her neighborhood. She doesn't have a PhD, and she has never written a play or recorded a CD. She doesn't even speak a foreign language. But, I sat in a ceremony where she was awarded a citywide humanitarian award for her service in Campbell Terrace. The local Human Relations Board was so impressed with her that they chose her to receive the award above many others in the community.

Campbell Terrace is a housing project in our community. The people who live there are mostly single moms and elderly women. Their greatest need is for assistance in making a difference in the lives of their children. Without intervention, many of the children get sucked into a life of drugs and crime. But what are mothers who live there to do? Life is hard and most of their hours are taken up trying to make ends meet. Role models are scarce. Enter Carolynne. She started a kids club on Fridays to help teach character and provide another voice of discipline and support to the children. When she ran into needs beyond her ability to personally handle, she recruited other men and women to help. When she found a single mother sleeping on the floor, she found someone who was giving away a bed to meet the need. Carolynne and her team did the same thing with old air conditioners and stoves, refrigerators and fans. Her example inspired men in the community to volunteer to change the oil in the cars of those who reside in the project. Every year she oversees a project to provide Christmas presents to every mother and child in Campbell Terrace.

Carloynne didn't feel she deserved the award and was shocked that she had been considered for the honor. What had moved the people to exalt her over all the others in the community was the fact that she did all of this with no strings attached. There was nothing these people could do for her, nothing tangible they could give in return. What Carolynne had done was love them—unconditionally! She had given herself and her time to them. In her mind, she already had her reward. She had gained the hearts of the people. They trusted her and loved her. She had earned their respect. Gang members, a very closed and protective group, had opened their hearts to her. She had influenced them to believe that life could be different. She was making a real difference in the lives of real people who were so radically different from her. Here was a middle class white lady from Canada helping change the lives of people in an inner city housing project in the South! And now, she had not only won the hearts of the residents, but the respect and honor of city officials.

The love inside your circle

What kind of love exists inside the circle of your personal relationships? Are you building your relationships on the shifting sand of self by only giving according to what you expect to receive? Take some time to take stock. Ask yourself the tough questions, and determine that you will be one of those people in life who are the "givers." At first, it is a frightful thought. What happens if no one loves you back? I am sure there will be those who take advantage of you along the way, and there will be some pain. But the self-seeking " loves" always end in pain. It's a guarantee. In this world that constantly says, "Give to me," people are looking for those who will show them genuine love. Folks, young and old, will always stay close to those who give without expecting to receive.

The benefit of unconditional love is that in some way, at some time, it will always come back to us. Jesus said, *"Give and it will be given to you. A good measure, pressed down, shaken together, and running over (I like the running over part!), will be poured into your lap. For with the measure you use, it will be measured to you."* (Luke 6:38) Let's increase the measure of the love we give to those in our circle of relationships. The more we truly give, the more we will be loved in return!

Questions for your relational journey

1. What is your definition of love? Is it only an emotion?

2. What does it mean that true love is unconditional?

3. Why are people so attracted to those who give love unconditionally?

4. What kind of love exists inside the circle of your personal relationships?

5. Why are people afraid to give (especially love) wIthout expecting anything in return?

Notes

1. What's Love God to Do With It-written by Terry Britten & Graham Lyle. Copyright © 1984 Capitol Records.
2. See John 3:16
3. See Romans 2:4

chapter 3

Faith

Believing more for someone than they do for themselves

But encourage one another daily, as long as
it is called Today, so that none of you may be
hardened through sin's deceitfulness.

Hebrews 3:13

Interestingly enough, according to the verse listed above, the best way to keep people from doing something wrong is not through warning or correction. The idea here is that daily encouragement and positive reinforcement is the way to motivate people to avoid evil. Sure, there is a place for warning and correction. After a person has spurned good and sound counsel, and begun to set out on a course leading to destruction, warning them is the right course of action. After they have ignored the warning, and the consequences of foolish behavior have come to light, a person should be corrected or rebuked. But the "bread and butter" way to motivate people to live better lives is through constant, daily encouragement.

How other's faith impacted my life

I grew up in a home with two great parents. Not only did they love me, but they believed in me and communicated that I could become anything I set my heart upon. They allowed my brothers, sister, and me to try new things in our attempt to explore our capabilities—art, sports, music lessons, etc. I even played junior varsity football in high school at 105 pounds soaking wet with pads on! Despite their support, I still grew up like many children, with low self-esteem. The sheer fact that I played football at my size shows that I craved acceptance among my peers. When I felt called to ministry, all my fears came to light. Ministry was what I was made for, but all my training was geared toward engineering. In high school, I took every math and science class I could. I saw liberal arts as weak. Then I realized that I was called to make my place in this world using language as my tool.

After sensing this new direction in my life, I told my pastor how terrified I was and how I wasn't cut out for the ministry. I listed all the reasons why this could not work. His response was simply, "Well then, I guess you qualify." His unspoken point being, ministry is not about you anyway. Even with his encouragement, I still feared that, in the end, I would fail.

During the time of my ministry training, the students I was studying alongside did not directly tell me that I "would never make it." They said it among themselves. They had reason to feel that way. I came into the group, a long-haired, hippy-looking kind of guy. I was younger than the rest and was extremely impetuous. I had cornered the market on pride and arrogance. To top it off, I wasn't a good speaker and showed little promise of improvement. In no way did I fit the standard pastor paradigm. And yet, eight years later I became their pastor! The other students had good reason to doubt my calling and bet against me, however during this time, three people had faith in me and changed my life.

Belief of a wife

As soon as Laura, then my girlfriend and now my wife, heard that I felt called to ministry she was behind me. She could see it! I was amazed. In short, she believed more for me than I did for myself. She was a constant source of encouragement. When doubts and fears crept in through my harmful comparison of myself against my peers, she was there to show me my future and set me back on course. She saw what I could and would become, and she treated me like I was already there! By this time, she already had my heart. But by having faith in me, she secured a place in my heart that no woman could take. She was more important than a girlfriend; she was a rudder and the wind in my sail. Her encouragement was a source of strength. She made me believe in myself. Insurmountable mountains became molehills as I saw myself through her eyes. She really believed I could do it! How could I live without such a person? Two and a half years later we were married. Today, she is still my rudder and my sail.

Belief of a friend

Jim Laffoon was my first mentor. He gave me a chance when others had no positive reinforcement to give. He talked with me of the future I hoped to have. It wasn't idle talk or wishful thinking. Jim saw something in me that I didn't see myself. Not only was he my mentor, but he made room for me in his life as a friend. He became a safe place in the competitive world of ministerial training. Because of that, I opened up to him and let him into my heart and life. Jim had "faith" for me and played a large role in shaping the early years of my ministry. He won my heart and in doing so, he impacted my life. "Michael, this is not your strongest area; you need to work on this." "Michael, your pride has blinded you to ___, and you have become judgmental." Jim saw all my crud, but with the eyes of faith, he saw what I could become. Today, though separated by many miles, Jim is as close to me as he was then. He captured my heart, because he believed more for me than I did for myself.

Belief of a pastor

Jerry Daley returned from a mission trip with a clear understanding that he was to move his family to Thailand and help start new churches in that land. Although he had a great staff of well-trained and competent people, Pastor Daley chose me, the youngest and least experienced of all, to be the new senior pastor of a church with 350 active members. Others on the staff and around the country quietly challenged him to think this through a little better. "The guy has potential, but at 26, with only three years experience, do you really think he is ready? What do you see in him?" Jerry always believed in me. From the first time I told him I felt called to ministry, he saw what I could not see in myself. And now, he was going to turn his life's work over to me. It worked! Today the church has grown to 3,000 members and we have started or helped to start dozens of other churches.

Jerry's time in Thailand did not go well, and he returned home sooner than expected. Many old friends saw this as a chance to point out his faults and criticize him for his "failures" but I never did because Jerry had captured my heart. He believed in me more than I had believed in myself, and in so doing he had gained my loyalty. To this day, Jerry Daley is my pastor. Over the years, due to the growth of our church and the ministries we have started, folks have encouraged me to break from the network of churches that Jerry leads and start my own. I steadfastly refused. Why? Was it blind loyalty? No way. By demonstrating real faith in me Jerry won a place in my heart, a place he continually keeps because he continues to express faith for my life.

Everyday challenges

Life is full of negativity. Everyday we are faced with things that challenge our confidence. Others climbing up the corporate ladder threaten to take our place and move us into vocational obscurity. Children and teens make harmful comparisons with peers, almost always leaving themselves on the short end of the proverbial stick. Self-help books are often no help and leave us, many times, with a clearer picture of what is wrong with us than how to make things right.

> When we see more for others than they do for themselves, we encourage them in the most basic of ways. We literally impart courage to them.

Pressures from work, home and school constantly picture for us what we have to do and how far we have to go; and they draw our focus to our obvious inadequacies. The result is that our confidence erodes, and we feel unprepared in light of the challenges that are ahead.

"Encourage" means to give courage. When we see more for others than they do for themselves, we encourage them in the most basic of ways. We literally impart courage to them. They are able to face what lies ahead with renewed confidence. The mountains get smaller as their focus shifts from inadequacy to possibility and from possibility to probability. Due to our encouragement, they begin to see things they had not seen before. They gain new perspectives, and they get new ideas. Their confidence builds as we become a fresh wind in their sagging sails.

Over time, the hearts of those you encourage begin to open to you. Trust begins to develop and love soon follows.

Remember this: People are drawn to those who believe in them. When you see another with God's eyes and speak to them from that vantage point you give them courage to keep going. That is exactly what happened to me in the illustrations I gave you from my own life. These people won my heart by believing in me and interacting with me from that vantage point.

> When you see another with God's eyes and speak to them from that vantage point you give them courage to keep going.

The power of faith to transform others

Alan Loy McGinnis, in his book *Bringing Out the Best in People*, beautifully illustrates the power of faith to transform others. He relates a now famous study performed by Psychologist Robert Rosenthal of Harvard University and a San Francisco school principal named Lenore Jacobson. The two devised a plot to test whether children perform poorly in the classroom because of the expectation, or the faith level, of the teacher. They tested every child in a particular school from kindergarten through fifth grade using a standardized test, withholding the true knowledge of the results from the teachers. Teachers were then secretly given the names of students, randomly chosen, who were supposed to be the future "cream of the crop." The teachers were totally unaware that the results were rigged. They actually supposed that these students, no matter how they presently performed, were destined to be the cream of the future crop. At the end of the year, all the students were tested again. The students who the teachers thought were the ones with the most potential, those whose names had been "leaked" to the teachers, scored far ahead of all the others, improving their scores by 15 to 27 I.Q. points! The only thing that changed in the classroom was the expectation, or the faith level, of the teachers for those particular children. What happened? These children had been given courage! Someone believed in them and it elevated them to a new level of performance.

Faith for those you love

The real question is this: in the lives of those you love, who is it that most commonly expresses faith for them? Who believes more for them than they do for themselves? Mark these people well, because they are in a position to win your loved one's hearts.

When parents begin to lose sight of the potential of their rebellious teen, they can be assured that others among their child's peer group will see a "future" for their son or daughter. What future will they see? Will it be helpful or harmful? Who do we want to be the rudder and the sail for our child? It doesn't take any relational skill to see a person as they are now, but it is quite another thing to see them as they could be. Dream of your child's potential. Without trying to caste them in some particular role, picture the kind of future they are capable of having. Then, without becoming pushy, during times when your child is down and discouraged, share your vision of the wonderful life you see for them. Always believe more for them than they do for themselves. No matter what is happening today, always keep your sight on a better tomorrow.

Who sees more for your spouse than they see for themselves? The boss? The cute co-worker? Or you? Our loved ones need to feel that there are those in their lives who believe in them even when they fail or when others out-perform them. Our loved ones need that place of safety where they can receive the courage they need to face another obstacle. Whoever gives them that courage will win their heart. Whoever continues to give them that courage will keep their heart.

> It doesn't take any relational skill to see a person as they are now, but it is quite another thing to see them as they could be.

Do you desire to begin a new friendship or to build on an existing one? Remember, everyone wants and needs someone in their life who believes in them. Become a person who believes in others. Begin to cultivate an image of a brighter future for those around you. Look beneath the surface in the lives of others. Look for the potential, the hidden talent. Learn to applaud the obvious. So many people are afraid that, if they applaud obvious talent in others, then pride will be the result.

I have a close friend who is tremendously talented musically. The story of his early childhood is sad. Those around him feared that too much encouragement would make him proud, so they gave him none. Instead, they praised him among themselves in whispers outside his hearing. It wasn't until he reached high school that he realized the depth of the talent that had been given him. By that time he was so filled with fear and insecurity that it took many years of healing (including a great wife and some encouraging friends) to propel him into the success that he is today. My friend's parents had the opportunity to propel him into a greater future but instead they chose to withhold their life-giving words. Each of us has that same opportunity to sow encouragement and life into those around us.

Everyone in your life needs and looks for those who will believe in them. Be that for those you love. Believe more for them than they believe for themselves. As we do this, their hearts will open more and more to us as time goes on.

Questions for your relational journey

1. What does it mean to have faith for another person, to believe more for them than they do for themselves?

2. Who has had faith for you at various points in your life?

3. How did that make you feel? How did those individuals having faith for you affect your life?

4. Why are people drawn to those who have faith for them?

5. Ask yourself, "Who is important to me in my life?" How do you demonstrate to them that you believe more for them than they do for themselves?

Interest

Placing value on what is important to others

Do nothing out of selfish ambition or vain
conceit, but in humility consider others better
than yourselves. Each of you should look not
only to your own interests, but also to the
interests of others.

Philippians 2:3-4

It seems that most advertising today is aimed at getting people
to "need" things they never thought they needed before.
Advertisers try to create in us the feeling that we will be missing
something or will somehow be less of a person without their
product. After all, movie stars and athletes use the product. If
we follow suit, we can be like them. Sales people use desire for
gain or fear of loss to motivate us to buy.

Frank Bettger was an undereducated and unsuccessful man
in his early years; but, as he wrote in his book, *How I Raised
Myself From Failure to Success in Selling*, Frank discovered
the secrets that eventually elevated him into becoming one
of the most successful insurance salesmen of his day. Frank
learned that selling people things they really didn't need was
a frustrating and unrewarding enterprise. Instead, he learned
to make a careful study of his client's needs and then tried to
help them meet those needs. To do this he had to listen and
truly be interested in the lives of the people to whom he was

selling. That lesson proved to be the beginning of what became a great American success story. Not only does this principle work in sales, but it is also a key to building healthy, lasting relationships.

Jesus our example

There was no greater example of this than Jesus. He left His place in heaven and came to earth to put our eternal interests above His own. The biblical quote at the beginning of this chapter shows the attitude that governed the way Christ lived among us. For us to further understand Christ's heart and attitude toward us, we need to continue reading in Philippians. *"Who, being in very nature God, did not consider equality with God something to be grasped, but made himself nothing, taking the very nature of a servant, being made in human likeness. And being found in appearance as a man, he humbled himself and became obedient to death—even death on a cross!"* (Philippians 2: 6-8)

He put aside that which would be in His own best interest, including self-preservation, all for the benefit of others. Over the years, He has won the hearts of millions upon millions of people. Beyond that, the next verse says that His Father *"...exalted Him to the highest place and gave Him the name that is above every name..."* (v 9) Who is more famous in the earth than Jesus Christ? Even those who reject Christianity admire Him for His lifestyle and teaching. And to think, His "career" lasted only three years and ended in death as a criminal! It is amazing how this principle works in winning and keeping the hearts of others.

A politician's interest in others

J. L. Dawkins always wanted to be in politics. He loved it, because he loved people. Everyone felt they were J. L.'s good buddy. He had a way of making you feel that way. He was interested in what interested other people and he listened to what they had to say. From sanitation workers to the city's wealthiest citizens, they all knew they had his ear. And it showed on election day. No one ever came close to unseating him. People didn't just vote for the Mayor, they voted for a friend. When the cancer started taking its toll on his body, the city began to memorialize him in ways that demonstrated the level of entrance he had won into their hearts. J. L., in the eyes of the city, was the picture of a true public servant.

Every politician would love such a relationship with constituents. How did J.L do it? He simply served others by being interested in what interested them. He could be found everywhere—talking to people, listening, laughing, and patting folks on the back for their achievement. Day in and day out he showed individuals that what concerned them concerned him; what made them laugh made him laugh; what seemed important to them became important to him. In the end, he was named "Mayor for Life."

The effect of interest and concern

The reality is that everyone is naturally attracted to what interests them. When we express an interest in what is important to others, we are showing interest in more than the thing itself. We are actually demonstrating interest in the person. By allowing others the opportunity to express their thoughts and desires with freedom, they slowly begin to open up. When we interact concerning the matter, we draw out of them that which is close to their heart. That is a gift. Many people live in homes, work in offices, and study in schools where they have little or no freedom to discuss the things closest to their hearts. When they find those who share a common interest, an immediate bond is often the result.

But what if you are a man and your wife is excited about needlework? Or what if your husband is into hunting and you can't stand the thought of killing Bambi? What if your teenager is into soccer (why can't he play real football)? How can a person be interested in something that is of no interest to them? Faking it isn't going to work, and you can't see your 6'4" frame in a chair for hours, fighting with needles. Nor is there any make-up on the market that goes with camouflage clothes!

> Many people live in homes, work in offices, and study in schools where they have little or no freedom to discuss the things closest to their hearts.

Go back to the beginning of the relationships you now enjoy. Think about how they began. You met that friend at work and the two of you clicked—same football team, same love of Mexican food, same terrible handicap in golf. You never even thought about owning a boat (seemed like a lot of trouble to you). But your buddy had a boat, and now you are standing in the grocery store in the magazine section looking at boats while your wife is searching for size three diapers. As you check out, you purchase a magazine that features your friend's boat. Giving you that sideways glance, your wife smiles at you, "You're so sweet. Bob will be excited to see that!" You don't really care all that much about boats, but Bob is a friend, and you do care about him. And he will care about you in return, because you have validated his passion for boating.

You hated art, but you spent hours walking through art museums during the time you dated that art major in college. She was excited about art, and you displayed your interest in her by giving attention to what was close to her heart. By doing this you showed her that she had a place in your heart, and as a consequence, you won a place in hers.

You don't have to buy a boat, learn to cross-stitch, take up art, or master bow hunting. When your wife is looking for a new pattern for a new project, go with her to the fabric store. When you get there, watch out for the guy sitting in the chair near the door rolling his eyes and looking bored. That fellow is sending a message to his wife that you don't want to send to yours. He is screaming in a thousand different ways, "I don't care about this!" What he doesn't realize is that she interprets that as, "In this area, you don't care about me!" She may be secure in other areas of their relationship but when it comes to this passion of hers, she'll never take the risk to open up to him. Instead, she'll find other people and give that piece of her heart to them. But this fellow is not you—oh no! You are right there, leaning over her shoulder, admiring her for the patience you obviously do not have, praising her for the generosity of her gift of time to make this for her sister's new baby. She turns, holds up two fabrics, and asks, "What do you think?" She isn't asking the lady who works there. She isn't asking the other woman looking through the solids. She is asking you, her friend, her husband, someone who values her by valuing what is important to her. What makes it even more special is that she knows that you really don't have any personal attraction toward sewing. She can only assume that you are there and involved because of the place she occupies in your heart. As you leave the store, you look over at the guy rolling his eyes by the door. Aren't you glad you aren't him? Your wife is glad. She's thrilled with the man she has, and she's impressed with how secure he is in his masculinity to be able to go through fabrics and discuss patterns with her. When you get into the car, you evaluate what that "gift" cost you—nothing. But what is the reward? A continued piece of your wife's heart—priceless!

People change and so do their interests. At every level we need to flow with them. Again, we don't have to develop brand new passions to match the passions of those we love. But, like Frank Bettger, we need to make a careful study of their continually changing needs and desires. Sit down with your spouse and ask questions. Talk to your children, inquiring about what makes them tick. Don't be satisfied with their initial answers. It may take a bit of time, but eventually, they will realize you really are interested in them, not just what makes them tick this month. Ask your clients where they plan to be in five years and how they plan to get there. Even if it has nothing to do with buying your product, listen to them describe how they plan to make their goals a reality.

Annie is six and has just discovered puzzles. Not the hard wooden ones—the real ones, made of cardboard. With great excitement, she showed me the scant progress she had made the night before. Laura and I were soon headed out the door for our morning run, but I had a few minutes while my wife finished moving the laundry into the dryer and rehearsing instructions given earlier to the older children. I lay on the floor and showed Annie the number one rule in puzzle assembly—find the corners first. Then I instructed her on the number two rule—segregate the straight edged pieces from the rest. She was thrilled. A whole new world of puzzle-making opened up to her. Soon she would break the 100-piece puzzle barrier and move into more complicated types. I hate puzzles. Even as a kid, I always considered them a waste of time. But I love Annie, and at least for this week, Annie loves puzzles. So there I was, on the floor, finding corners and straight edges, until I was admonished by the "outside voice" coming from the little six-year-old mouth, "Dad, don't do the whole thing!" When I returned home from the run, I was the first to be greeted with the news of her progress. She thinks I am "the man!" I took a few minutes to do something I don't enjoy. The reward? A continued piece of a little girl's heart.

I am convinced that no one has to live a friendless existence. People are everywhere, and wherever there are people, there are passions that occupy their attention and time. All we have to do is find people and start asking them questions. Once we strike upon the topic of their passion, their mouth will generally open followed closely by their heart. When you explore those areas of their lives with them, you serve people by putting their interests above your own. If it is a new relationship, you are putting yourself in a position to win their heart. If it is an existing relationship you are building upon what you already have.

Why let co-workers and friends care more about our loved ones than we do? Why let the unsavory gal who works across the hall have an inroad into the heart of your husband, just because you decided that taking the time to show interest in him was too much effort? Why let peers capture the hearts of our children, because our lives are too busy to find puzzle corners or learn what pedal pushers are?

As we value others by taking an interest in what is important to them we will touch their hearts. Those who apply this key and consistently put others' interests before their own will be some of the richest people relationally. Put this into practice in your own life and you will never be in want for friends and family.

Questions for your relational journey

1. In your top three relationships, what are the main interests of those people? List at least three per person. Do you regularly demonstrate interest in those things?

2. How do people communicate their passions and interests? How can we discover the passions and interests of those we love?

3. Do we have to learn to love the same things as others in order to be successful in our relationships with them? How then can we show interest in something that does not naturally interest us?

4. What happens inside the hearts of others when we do that? Why are they attracted to us?

chapter 5

Availability

Making room for others in crisis and in life

A new command I give you; Love one another. As
I have loved you, so you must love one another.

John 13:34

Carry each other's burdens, and in this way you
will fulfill the law of Christ.

Galatians 6:2

There is no doubt that everyone in this life will experience pain.
All of us have had and will continue to have some type of pain
occur in our lives. I wish it weren't true. Being in pain is bad
enough, but being in pain alone is almost unbearable. I was
experiencing a revisitation of what seemed to be all I had eaten
for the last year at one end, and Montezuma's revenge (why
did he hate me so?) at the other end, in the wee hours of the
morning. All alone in the dorm during Bible College, cleaning
up my own mess, I resolved that these guys may be great guys,
but being sick among them was a real drag. The next morning,
I called my mother who was all too glad to take me in and nurse
me to health. Upon arriving at home, my body continued to test
the limits of viral assault, but I can't tell you how much better I
felt inside. Here, in my old bed, I was comforted that she was
in this thing with me to the end. Two days later I was back at
the grind, more firmly convinced that no one could take mom's
place. I would always be her boy (a fact I sometimes regretted

later in life when, at 30, she was still telling me it was too cold to go out without a hat), and she would always be Mom.

A new commandment

Some people have wondered what Jesus meant when He told His followers that He was giving them a new commandment. Wasn't it the same as the old commandment? Jesus Himself had said that the greatest commandment was to "...*love the Lord your God with all your heart and with all your soul and with all your mind. And the second is like it; Love your neighbor as yourself.*" (Matthew 22:37,39) But now He says He is giving them a new commandment. What's new about it? Notice in the commandment drawn from the Old Testament that we are told to love our neighbor as *ourselves.* Now He is telling them to love others as they have been loved by Him. How is it that we have been loved by God? Paul told the Roman believers that "...*God demonstrates His own love for us in this: While we were still sinners, Christ died for us.*" (Romans 5:8) The point is that when we were in the greatest crisis of all and unable to help ourselves, Jesus Christ laid down His life for us. He loved us by reaching us in the midst of our greatest need, even though we had no appetite for Him or His ways. Before we could search, before we knew to search, He was there. It was a sacrificial love—the kind that makes itself available to people in need, the kind that sees it through to the end. From now on, as the commandment goes, we are to love others like that.

The principle of availability

I call this the principle of availability. Many people claim to be available to their loved ones. I've heard people say, "He knows I am available to him. He can call on me whenever he wants." But I am talking about something much deeper than that. I'm talking about making people a priority; about being there when the chips are down. This is about seeing them through their crisis.

Joby Adams was a perfect example of this. I can't tell you the number of times when we were together, that he had to stop to check on a person or to see how someone was doing. He knew everything about people's situations. He knew that Mrs. So-and-So was a neighbor of Mr. Something, who used to work with his dad until her divorce, and that she had lost the house. Her oldest son died of cancer a couple of years ago, and she has been alone ever since. Joby ran into Mr. Something at the mall last week and learned that Mrs. So-and-So had asked about him, so on the way back into town, we had to stop for just a minute. Mrs. Old Friend was also there, so we better go inside and see how everyone is doing. "How are you doing? And your son? Did he finish at State? Is he working nearby? When was the accident?" Before we were done, he was rubbing both ladies on the arm saying, "Bless your heart, bless your heart," and fighting back tears. He was always there, always concerned, always a friend, and people loved him for it. They stood in line forever at his funeral, each thinking of themselves as a special friend of Joby. He had been there for them as a friend when they needed him, and now they were there to demonstrate their affection for him. He had won their hearts by loving them as he had been loved by God. Joby made people a priority and they let him into their hearts and lives.

A crisis takes time

A deep and lasting bond is established between people who

go through tough times together. In the crucible of crisis, people are forced to depend on others at a level they would normally be uncomfortable with. Tears once shed in secret are now the waters that flow for the privileged few to see. Advice never before sought is now asked for with a heart desperately looking for wisdom. The people who are holding your hand when the runaway comes through the door, or bringing you coffee at the late night vigil beside the sick bed, are the ones you often share the longest and deepest connection. Those who show up to rake the yard and mend the fence after your back surgery are often the ones you remember through the years with the fondest of memories.

> A deep and lasting bond is established between people who go through tough times together.

Many people are too busy to take the time it requires to be there for someone else. No one ever has a crisis on schedule. It is never a good time. On top of that, a crisis takes time—time we often don't have, and certainly time no one could have had the foresight to factor in. When people pass by on the other side of the road, as the Priests and Levites did in the Biblical story of the Good Samaritan[1], they can be assured that someone else in life will take their place and nurse their hurting friend back to health. At the same time, they should recognize that they have passed up more than a crisis. They have given away an opportunity to demonstrate love of a divine type and, thereby, build or deepen a heart tie with a person who will love them for it.

Recognizing the crisis

The biggest problem we have, however, is not pulling away

from life to give proper attention to those in crisis. Our greatest problem comes in recognizing a crisis when it has arisen. The examples I have already listed are obvious and easy to spot, but most crises are not plainly discerned. Missing these is where the greatest damage is done. Our trouble lies in the fact that we like to be the ones who define what constitutes a true crisis. We look at the circumstances and evaluate

> A crisis is defined as such by the person who is in it.

them by our own set of strengths and weaknesses or our personal station in life. If we discern that the person is at fault for bringing this upon himself or herself, we might be slower or more hesitant to reach out with compassion. In reality, a crisis is defined as such by the person who is in it. Often what constitutes a crisis is not the thing itself, but how one feels about it at the time. To them, at that moment, it is a crisis, even though it is clear to you that it's not.

Let me illustrate. Your nine-year-old daughter just found out that her best friend lied about her to the other students in her class. She is devastated. This was her *best* friend! Being the dramatic type, it hits her even harder. She comes into the house oblivious to the fact that you are deeply engrossed in trying to pay the bills with a checkbook that just won't balance. She goes on and on concerning something about friends and school, crying and talking, crying and talking. "Honey, go wash your face. You'll feel better then. I can't deal with this right now." After washing her face and not feeling any better, she goes into your bedroom and calls another friend who is glad to walk her through it. After dinner, she asks if she can spend the night with her confidant. Off she goes with your permission.

You knew she'd feel better if she washed her face. You gave away an opportunity to be her knight in shining armor and sent her off to cry on the shoulder of the little girl down the street.

Winning and keeping the hearts of others requires that we make ourselves available to those we love. When we do this, we communicate the place of priority they hold in our lives. Once they realize they have that place, they will defend the relationship with everything they have. You will defend a friend who has been in the trenches with you from the attack of hostile co-workers, even though it means taking some heat yourself. You don't mind standing up for those who stood up for you in your time of trouble.

The same holds true in relationships that are harmful. When Julie was cut from the cheerleading squad, dad figured it was because she didn't really give it her all. "She has always had a problem with that," he reasons, "Besides, she needs to concentrate more on academics anyway." It is a shame dad didn't read the previous chapter. Had he, he might have taken the time to find out that becoming a cheerleader has been a dream of Julie's. Eventually, all her disappointment would have come pouring out, and he would have been able to share a piece of his life story with her. It wasn't cheerleading, but it was football and it hurt when his friends made the team, but he was let go. He could have shared with her the comfort that eventually came to him, but he passed up the opportunity, because he didn't think it was a real crisis. Now, instead of being in the safe arms of her father, she is in the arms of a boy from school who feels that she should have made the team. She has the talent. She has the looks. He's been watching her. Later when dad finally realizes that this relationship has become physical and is destructive, Julie fights him tooth and nail. She loves this boy. He understands her. It's too bad dad didn't discern the crisis that was before him when he had the chance. It's too bad he opted to define the crisis himself, instead of letting Julie define it, and then respond accordingly to her. I'm not blaming dad for Julie's decline into moral failure. She made her own bad choices. I am blaming him for leaving her vulnerable when he had the chance to deeply touch his daughter, when she needed him most.

I wonder how many spouses wandered off into extra-marital affairs, because, in needing someone to talk to, they found the wrong person, because their spouse wasn't there. How many people have allowed good friendships to erode, because they weren't there in their friend's time of need? In each of these cases and others like them, someone will come along side and be there for those in need. These are the ones who are in a position to capture the heart and win the person.

I am not contending for being jerked around by those who, with unbridled emotion, are seeking attention by going from one supposed crisis to another. Unfortunately, these poor souls will become known for the actors they are, and they will suffer without support in times of true need, as a consequence of continually "crying wolf" when there is no "wolf."

We live in a world where everything fights for our time. If we are to truly value others, we must etch out time for them. We do that by dropping lesser things for more important things, and by being there for them in the midst of their crisis, as they define crisis. Whoever does this is in a position to greatly impact the hearts of those around them.

Questions for your relational journey

1. Who has "been there" for you in your life when the chips were down? Describe your feelings toward those people. Why do you feel that way?

2. Do the people in your life know that they are a priority to you? How do they know that? How have you demonstrated that to them?

3. When was the last time you "held the hand" of someone as you walked with them through a time of crisis?

4. What is a crisis? Who should define what a crisis is?

5. Have you ever met people who used "crisis" situations to get attention? How can you tell the real from the exaggerated?

Notes

1. See Luke 10:30-36

chapter 6

Respect

Establishing a person's worth

Give everyone what you owe him...
If respect, then respect; if honor, then honor.

Romans 13:7

I have a friend who now travels the world as a much sought-after speaker and a leader in a large and growing network of churches. People love him. His personality is magnetic. Once while traveling on a speaking trip through the same area of the country, I was privileged to be hosted by some of the same folks who had hosted him just months before. I heard housewife after housewife talk about how he called ahead in preparation for his arrival and "put his order in" for a certain type of homemade cookie or special desert. And they loved it! I knew I could never pull that off. People remembered his messages because they remembered him. He had worked his way into their hearts, and they eagerly anticipated his return.

Through close personal contact over the years I have had occasion, first hand, to observe my friend at work. I marveled at his magnetism and wondered how it worked. It had to be more than personality alone. It first became clear when I heard him talking about other people—people we both knew. I had considered these folks ordinary people, with no outstanding qualities; but not this fellow. When he spoke of people, I saw them in a different light. He had given them honor, and respect. You could tell it in his voice. He thought they were really something. Small things stood out to him. Not only did he subtly convey his honor of these people to me, but he had also done so to them. I wasn't the only one who felt it—they had felt it too, and they loved him for it.

Reflecting on my association with him, I saw that he had done the same with me on numerous occasions. A wonderful speaker himself, he needed no help from anyone, least of all me. I hate to be interrupted when I am preparing for a sermon—it breaks my concentration and disrupts my "flow." But time and again over the years, I have instructed my secretary to put his call through, so he could ask me about some obscure statistic he could not put his hands on. The conversation never stopped there, and I never minded. He would go on to ask me about this or that or my opinion on something happening in the world. Occasionally, he would ask about a situation he was facing, seeking my insight. I could tell he respected my ideas, and in respecting my ideas, he respected me. He did that with everybody, and that is why people let him into their hearts.

The necessity of respect

For too many, however, respect is something only given to those who have climbed higher on the ladder of life than themselves. To the layman, the medical student has a wealth of knowledge, but compared to a surgeon, the medical student has miles to go. Most of the people on the street would afford the medical student a fair measure of respect, simply because he was able to get into medical school. But most would not expect the surgeon to give the student another thought, since he is so far down the medical ladder. We give the boss respect. We have to—he is the boss. But, we do not give respect to co-workers, because they are on the same rung as we are.

We expect honor and respect, but we are very cautious and stingy in giving it out. We fear that if we grant honor to those near us on the social, educational, or economic ladder, it will somehow weaken our position or give the other fellow a "big head." We, in turn, will seem smaller and less significant, since he will then feel free to see himself better than us. Each of us yearns to be noticed

> The need for acceptance and approval are basic to human existence.

by others, to have people acknowledge and value us for who we are. I believe that the need for acceptance and approval are basic to human existence. Everyone, universally, craves these things. Those who satisfy this basic drive are the ones who will change lives.

The secret to my friend's magnetism was simply that he felt free to give respect to people no matter their station on the ladder. First, he didn't make himself the measure. He wasn't concerned about who was ahead or who was behind. Second, he always found something of value in almost everyone he met. People perceived that he saw them as they saw themselves. They were acknowledged. Then he pulled them up to a status of respect higher than what most people afforded them. They were valued. True respect is so rarely offered to most people, so they are irresistibly drawn to those from whom it comes.

How respect turned rebellious hearts

The academy teachers and administrators regretted their decision to extend the school into the upper grades. If it had been one stray rebel or a few scattered among the crowd, it would have been one thing; but, by the time I came along, they had developed a group dynamic. I was armed with a love for them and one single truth. Treat the junior high kids like high school kids, and treat the high school kids like college-aged kids, and you'll see remarkable changes in their behavior and in their response to you. At first, they came to my meetings because they wanted to hang out together, and they were made to come by their parents. But my wife and I put into practice what little we knew. Looking back, the meetings were terrible. I'm glad they weren't video taped. (Had they been, the tapes could be used to torture political prisoners!) But they kept coming and hanging out in our apartment. When I drove my little green Volkswagen bug through the parking lot, they would often surround it and not let me pass, standing on the bumper or piling into the available seats. (Did you know that 10 teenagers can actually fit into the back seat of a VW bug?) They loved us!

One day, I noticed through the window of one of the buildings that an administrator was walking into one of the classrooms filled with my students. After a while he didn't emerge. I knew that meant trouble, so I left my place and went to see what they had gotten into now. When I walked into the room it was clear that the battle lines had been drawn. Later a group of students stood around me, thanking me for coming. "When you walked in," they said, "we felt like the cavalry had arrived!" What had we done to receive such a place in their hearts? We respected them, even though they were beneath us in station and age, and even though their behavior sometimes created trouble.

But, and this is key, we didn't respect them without merit. I made them my tutors on contemporary culture. I asked them to help me select the type of fun stuff we should do. I joked with the guys about sports stuff as if they were my equals in life. Laura sat on the couch watching movies with the girls. They were part of our family. We valued their opinions and sought their ideas about things. But most of all, we listened to them, really listened. Even when we disagreed, we did not just write them off as ignorant or rebellious teens. We interacted. Our interaction, our listening to them validated them. In effect, rather than talking down to them, we pulled them up on the ladder, sat down on a common rung and talked.

How do we treat those around us?

When the air conditioning repairman comes to your house, how do you treat him? Do you evaluate him according to his financial station relative to yours? Or do you treat him as an equal because he is a human? Further, you should respect him for the expert he is. If you had known what to do with your air conditioner, you would never have called for his assistance. Give him the place he has earned and treat him as your superior in this arena, granting him the respect he deserves.

Have you ever been in the army? If not, then the nineteen-year-old PFC has done something you have not. Honor him for his commitment to his nation, treating him with respect for the service he has rendered and the accomplishment of making it to PFC. When dining in a restaurant, do you plan to converse with the cook concerning your order and enter the kitchen to obtain your food when it is ready? Then respect the waitress for the service she provides. She is doing what you would not do. Don't evaluate her by your station in life. Don't measure her socially, educationally, or economically. Value her because she is human and respect her for the job she does.

This idea is powerful! Take another look at your children. They have areas of expertise that far exceed your personal skill level. When was the last time you attended a high school gym class? Things are different now than when you were in school. Don't try to be the family high school expert. Your opinion on a certain subject is valid, but so is the opinion of a child, friend, or spouse who sees a different point of view. Give them the place you require for yourself, the honor of having an opinion. As a parent, you don't have to abrogate your role, setting aside your place as the authority in the home in order to discuss *The Rise and Fall of the Roman Empire* with your teenage children. Your ideas on drugs and pre-marital sex should carry the day, but not every topic is so weighty. You might ask your nine-year-old, instead of his coach, what "off-sides" means during his soccer match. You might break out the map and discuss alternate routes with your teenage child while on a family vacation.

My two older girls are great dancers, and my wife is a natural, but she is not as trained as they are. I will find them in the kitchen or the hallway, arms outstretched in some position called by some French name, passing on some new step to their mother, all initiated by Mom. "Okay, show me again," and away they go. (They just run me out of the room and laugh when I give it a shot.) My wife is allowing the taught-one to become the teacher. In so doing, she is giving respect and keeping the place she has in their hearts. Respect is a statement of a person's value, and people always stay close to those who regularly give them the honor they desire.

We are surrounded by people who have had experiences we have not had, and who have learned things we have not learned. They are experts on the topic of their own lives, and there is tremendous value in that. If a co-worker has been on a trip to a part of the world you have not seen, let her be the expert. Don't quote everything you've ever read in *Reader's Digest* on the subject. In fact, take another step. Ask questions—with interest. Make it personal. On several occasions, I have asked a waitress for her opinion during a discussion I was having with others at the table. More than once I have been impressed with the response. But more importantly, I have given a gift.

> Respect is a statement of a person's value, and people always stay close to those who regularly give them the honor they desire.

Who said a spouse or a friend has to have the same training or experience as you, to make valid input into your vocational situation? Chances are, whatever you do has something, at some level, to do with people. Although you know your job, certainly you wouldn't claim to have cornered the market on people skills. More importantly, others may not know all about the matters pertaining to your job, but they do know you. Another perspective on you might be helpful. People sometimes say to me, "I don't want to tell you how to do your job but …" To which I reply, "Please tell me how to do my job!" It's true, I have been doing my job for over twenty years, but

I can't begin to count the insights I have gleaned from someone with a great idea.

You can begin today to cultivate a new magnetism in your life. Look for things in those you love that are worthy of respect. Seek for ways to honor people. Decide to acknowledge that every person you meet has something in his or her life that could benefit you. Determine now that you will reject the impulse to be the expert, and that you will reject the idea that you must defend your rung on the ladder by withholding honor and respect from those around or beneath you. Hearts will open in new ways and at deeper levels as you apply this principle at home, at work, and at play.

Questions for your relational journey

1. Is it possible to respect people who are considered by most to be "average?" Name some "average" people in your life and outline why you respect them.

2. What happens in a person's heart when we afford them the respect they crave but others rarely give?

3. How do you treat people who occupy space on a lower rung on the economic, educational, or social ladder of life than you? Do such things matter to you? Should they? Why do we tend to evaluate people's worth according to their "station"?

4. Why are people attracted to those who give them respect?

chapter 7

Time
The key to unlocking a heart

There is a time for everything, and a season for every activity under heaven:

Ecclesiastes 3:1

See then that you walk circumspectly, not as fools but as wise, redeeming the time, because the days are evil.

Ephesians 5:15-16 (NKJV)

Young or old, rich or poor, male or female, we all share one thing in common. Each person on the face of the earth shares the same allotment of time—60 seconds in every minute, 60 minutes in every hour, 24 hours in every day, and 365 days a year. We also share the same funny ideas about time. We talk about saving time, but no bank stores minutes to be used on another day. We say we don't have time, but each of us has twenty-four hours in every day. The truth is, we really don't understand time, and so we easily mismanage our lives in relation to it. Make no mistake—time is a powerful thing.

I am of the personal conviction that our relationships are the most important things in life. Our happiness on earth will be governed by those relationships, and our future will be shaped by them.

The way we manage our lives in relation to time will determine the quality of our relationships. We may say we value our daughter and would even die for her, but she has her doubts when, although willing to pay for ballet lessons, we never make it to the recitals. We may claim that our children are important and that all our hard work is for them, but if they are raised by day care workers rather than us, we shouldn't be surprised when, as teenagers, their deepest loyalties reside outside the home. People are full of trite platitudes as to what is important to them; however, talk is cheap. The real measure of what we value is how we live our lives in relation to time. How do we use that twenty-four hours a day? Say what you like about the intentions of your heart, but how you spend your time dictates what you really are.

> The real measure of what we value is how we live our lives in relation to time.

Time is life

Underscore this—your time is your life! As your time goes, so goes your life. The allocation of your time determines your priorities. When your hobbies get most of your spare time instead of your spouse, it is clear to them (and others as well) that you value it over them. In reality, since the hobby is designed for your personal pleasure, it isn't really the hobby that is valued over your spouse but yourself! The only way for people to be a priority in your life is for them to have a portion of your time. You only have so much time, so when you spend time with a person, you are making a statement of their value. You establish them as important. Actions speak louder then words, as the old saying goes, and how you spend your time is the yardstick of what you truly treasure.

As I have already said, your time is your life, and your priorities determine what is important to you and the direction of your heart. Therefore, whomever you spend time with is in a position to influence your heart, both positively and negatively.

I recently returned from a speaking trip to Africa. One of the other speakers at the convention, a friend of mine, brought his two oldest children with him. The idea was to see some of East Africa together and spend quality time before his son and daughter went off to college. After he finished his part, this popular and very busy leader was off to Lake Victoria for a tour. Prior to leaving, I remarked how I enjoyed spending time with such great children, to which he quickly replied, "It's not hard to raise great kids." How perfectly he illustrated my point! The reason he had such great kids is that he had so clearly made them a priority in his life. In giving his time to them, he had given his heart and established their value. In return, they had given their hearts to him.

> Whomever you spend time with is in a position to influence your heart, both positively and negatively.

Your heart goes where your time goes. Not only does this work for our good but also to our detriment. When we spend time with people of the opposite sex to whom we are not married, we are putting ourselves in a dangerous place.

The negative effect of time on a relationship

It always starts innocently—a male boss and his female secretary burning the midnight oil to get that project in on time. The first night they order out for Chinese food. The next night they heat up something she "threw together" at home, anticipating another late night. There is no sexual attraction. He is grateful for her diligent service, and she admires his strong leadership. Over dinner each night they converse about the strengths and weaknesses of their respective marriages. No one's marriage is perfect. Soon her heart goes out to him and his to her. He hugs her goodnight and she hugs him back. As they part, they linger, staying close, and then he does it. He kisses her. And that begins it. What started out as a seemingly innocent project at work, winds up in an extra-marital affair that destroys two families. All involved had underestimated the power of spending time alone with another. I am not saying that time spent alone with a member of the opposite sex will always result in a sexual relationship, but this scene has been played out far too many times to ignore the power of this principle.

> I am not saying that time spent alone with a member of the opposite sex will always result in a sexual relationship, but this scene has been played out far too many times to ignore the power of this principle.

Sometimes nothing sexual happens at all. Sometimes it ends with his heart going out to her and/or her heart going out to him. Some call this an emotional affair, nothing physical, just the excitement of getting emotional needs met by someone other than your spouse. Even though nothing physically inappropriate occurs, emotional affairs damage marriages as well. It is obvious that a marriage is built around the heart. When your heart goes out to a person, it belongs to that person. If that person is someone other than your spouse, then you are destroying your marriage from the inside out. The delight you give the other person isn't theirs, it belongs to your spouse.

The attention you pay to them doesn't belong to them; it should go to your spouse. The affection you display belongs not to that co-worker but to your spouse. Brick by brick you are dismantling the emotional fortress that was or should be your marriage, and you are weakening it from within. Even if the emotional affair never becomes physical, the damage is done. You have given your heart away.

The positive effect of time to build up relationships

Time spent alone can build up as well as tear down. My wife teaches our children at home, and she does a great job. Our three oldest are in college on academic scholarships. But even after seventeen years of home-educating our children, the pressure is still there. My responsibilities have broadened and brought new pressure into our family as well. As our children get older, their activities multiply, and scheduling has become a nightmare. On top of that, Laura is being called upon more to speak and share in various settings. But, we are doing even better as a family, and Laura and I are connected more deeply now than ever before in our marriage. Laura has been running each morning for years. It keeps her healthy and provides tremendous stress relief. Six years ago, I began to run with her. Rain or shine, hot or cold, we spend one hour together on the road each day. On our day off, we culminate our run with breakfast. By no means are we setting any speed records—it is connection time. We talk the whole time (except for hills!). This time alone has bonded us together, bolstered our communication, and enabled us to thrive in this period of our lives.

Time alone while dating

Ted was in love with the girl of his dreams and I was warning him about the dangers of time alone. "Don't trust yourself. Time alone puts you in a dangerous position. First, your heart goes out, then your hormones, then your head, in that order. By the time your head catches up with your heart and your hormones, it will be too late." He didn't listen and he ruined what could have been a wonderful relationship. Now I admit, I am old-fashioned. I believe in courtship and think dating is a bad idea. As a society, we would never let a sixteen year old carry around a gun (too dangerous) or drink alcohol (destructive). We even limit when and where they can drive. We monitor who they hang out with and insist on a reasonable time to be home. But we will send them out alone with the opposite sex for three hours of unsupervised time. Their heart is already gone, their hormones constantly raging, and we sit at home in peace, reading the paper, as our child tries in vain to deny the natural urges within. They can't help it! They were made that way! But they were also given two parents to guide them through this time in their life.

> A young person can live a wonderful, healthy life without playing Russian roulette with morality in the modern dating game.

Our local newspaper reported just yesterday that, according to a national survey, 1 in 5 girls are subject to being molested while on a date! That is a 20% chance! If you knew that your child had a 20% chance of being shot while walking through a certain neighborhood, you wouldn't even let them out of the house. That 20% only counts those who say "no" but are forced. The survey has no reference to those who, while on a date, say "yes!" How much damage has been done during unsupervised time alone with members of the opposite sex! I don't care what standard contemporary culture dictates. A young person can live a wonderful, healthy life without playing Russian roulette with morality in the modern dating game. Laura's parents insisted that we "date" on the couch in their living room. We spent time with her family and in activities with other people. We had a great time at sporting events and with friends. I went on vacations with her family and she with mine. As a result, I grew close to her whole family, and we are still close. Laura's father, a retired army Lt. Colonel, serves on my staff.

The great investment

When you give your time to someone, you are investing your life. Invest well. Time spent in front of the television doesn't count as family time, but time wrestling on the floor with the boys does. What ever happened to meals together? Some things are worth fighting for. I appreciate the attitude my older children have on this score. They like hanging out with friends like anyone else, but we have tried to model the value of time together for them by giving our time to them. When called upon to sacrifice their activities for the sake of family continuity, they gladly comply. Does investment in family pay dividends? Last night my three oldest sons (we have eight children) ages 16, 18, and 20, hatched an idea. They wanted to go to the movies with their mother and father. My two oldest daughters thought that was a great idea and offered to watch the younger ones. How many young men want to hang out with their parents? I call that a dividend!

Where am I going to find all the time I need to invest in my spouse, children, parents, siblings, friends, boss, co-workers, and clients? Remember, we all have the same amount of time. It all depends on how we break it up. Most of what happens in our lives just happens; we don't plan it. Often, we commit to this or that without counting the cost in terms of its demands on our time. Before we know it, our lives are pulled in so many directions we can't even keep up. Then we read a chapter like this one, and we feel even more out of control. One place to start is with the time we spend on ourselves. I have known people who say they have no time for their family but can always find time for that hobby or a round of golf. Others never have the time for a date with their spouse, but they always have time to work overtime to earn a few extra bucks. We can't miss the evening news, and reading the morning paper is a sacred rite.

Sometimes we have to set aside the lesser things for the important things. With my schedule, my time is really tight, but I have determined to be a family man, not just in word, but in deed. I used to be a pretty fair tennis player but I haven't hit a ball in years. I traded it in for our kids' soccer matches and breakfast with my wife. I get my exercise with my wife, and a majority of my friends don't play tennis anyway. Major on others and minor on self. The reward always outweighs the sacrifice!

Your time investment plan

So, how can we manage ourselves better in relation to time to maximize our investment in others? Why not stop right now and take stock. A few pointers might help with our reflection:

1. Who is really important to you? Rank them. Is your boss more important to you than your spouse? Are your clients or co-workers more valuable to you than your children?

2. What is most important to those we love? Time put into those activities will yield the highest returns in terms of communicating value to our loved ones. Attending a play with your theater-loving wife will produce greater results than watching the Twins beat the Red Sox.

3. What allocations of time do we have already in place that, if maximized, will yield greater results? If your husband takes your son to soccer matches on Saturdays, why not make it a family affair? When you put the children to bed, how about telling a short story from your childhood? When you are running errands, swing by a friend's house and invite them along.

4. What potentially dangerous traps, created by time alone with others, should we avoid? Are we in the habit of eating lunch alone with co-workers of the opposite sex? Is there a person at work toward whom we are attracted?

As with our personal finances, we need a time investment plan. Begin now to readjust your expenditures of the clock to reap relational dividends.

Questions for your relational journey

1. It has been said that love is a four-lettered word spelled "t-i-m-e." Is this true? Why or why not?

2. The real measure of what we value is how we live our lives in relation to time. What do you truly value? How does your allotment of time to that person or activity back that up?

3. When we spend time with people we are putting them into a position to capture our hearts, and us in turn, to capture theirs. How has this been true in your own life?

4. An "emotional affair" is destructive to a marriage. Why?

5. Not all time spent in activity with others is of the same quality. What kinds of activities yield the best return?

chapter 8

Communication

The lifeline to every relationship

Let no unwholesome word proceed from your mouth, but only such a word as is good for edification according to the need of the moment, that it may give grace to those who hear.

Ephesians 4:29 (NASB)

Cindy had taken all she was going to take. Harold had pushed her over the edge with his last comment. She knew what she had to do—he would never let her escape if she tried to just walk out the door. She bought tickets to a game to be played two weeks away and presented them to him at dinner. He thought they were to attend the game together but the ruse was designed to throw him off course. Three days later, expecting nothing, Harold came home to a house that was now only partially furnished. Pictures of the children and all her clothes were also missing. Cindy had moved it all into an apartment across town. She never returned home.

I asked Cindy what had happened to make her so resolute in her decision, and so determined in her course of action. She told me that one morning prior to parting for work, she mentioned their pending wedding anniversary to Harold in the midst of a heated argument. She couldn't believe Harold's response. When he said what he said, she was sure that, despite what he told her, he really didn't love her. She realized then that their marriage was dead and without hope. She felt like a fool for not realizing it sooner. What had Harold said? In an effort to score a few points in the argument, Harold opened the door and just before stepping over the threshold to leave, said to his wife, "What anniversary? We don't even have a marriage to celebrate!"

> Words can do more than hurt us—words can destroy us.

Feeling triumphant, he closed the door behind him and drove off to work. In reality, he drove off more than the car; these cutting words proved to be "the straw that broke the camel's back."

Growing up, I often heard well-meaning people try to administer self-comfort by passing on this over-used rhyme. "Sticks and stones can break my bones but words will never hurt me." How many children have quoted that line to a playground antagonist? Words can do more damage than any rock or stick has ever inflicted.

Words are powerful things. Words, skillfully put together, have galvanized the hearts of the masses and mobilized whole nations, to the end that they even send their sons to war. Words have been used to convey the magic of love that opens the soul and steals the heart of another. Loved ones wait with bated breath outside the emergency room hoping for the words, "He made it," while fearing the words, "I'm sorry. We did all we could." Words can do more than hurt us—words can destroy us. Words can also build up and make us great. Make no mistake—words are powerful things.

Encouraging words—a lifeline

In the middle of the 20th century, Navy divers were used to save lives and salvage wreckage. Salvage diving was a dangerous profession that required daring men to risk their lives in the deep sea. There exist some striking similarities between salvage diving and the building of successful relationships. Divers are lowered into the sea by a cable, clothed in large pressurized suits. They descend to the bottom aided by lead-weighted shoes. Once on the bottom, divers do their work and are totally dependent upon one very important tube that runs from the ship to the suit. This tube is their lifeline, carrying a mixture of gases necessary to sustain human life, and enabling the diver to continue in his work. Cut the line, and the diver will soon die. Relationships are also sustained by one simple lifeline—communication. Without communication relationships also die. Every relationship is totally dependent on communication to continue its existence. In fact, each of the six points already mentioned is built on the foundation of this one simple, but profound, truth. If we want to develop successful relationships by winning and keeping the hearts of others, we need to master the art of communication. Love, faith, interest, availability, and respect must all be shared in some way, and time provides the opportunity to communicate each one of these vital keys. Without a doubt, communication is the lifeline of relationships.

The quality of communication

But not all communication is helpful. In fact, as we have already discussed, some types of communication are harmful. The real point at issue with the diver is not just having a tube, but the quality of what passes through it. If nothing is flowing through the tube at all, one wonders why it is even connected. The same holds true with relationships. If there is no communication at all, one wonders if a real relationship even exists. But assuming that something is passing through the tube, the quality of the mixture must be monitored. One might suppose that pure oxygen is pushed into the suit of the diver, but that would be incorrect. We, on the surface, do not breathe pure oxygen, but we breathe a combination of gasses found naturally in the atmosphere. We are very sensitive creatures. Too much carbon dioxide or too much oxygen and the diver could suffer irreparable damage! That same ideal mixture that we enjoy on the surface must be provided to the diver, so the quality of what passes through the tube is vital to the life of the man below. In a similar way, the quality of our relationships is totally dependent on the quality of what passes through the lifeline of communication.

Putrid communication

In the Bible, Paul the Apostle instructed believers on this topic with the following admonition: *"Let no unwholesome word proceed from your mouth, but only such a word as is good for edification according to the need of the moment, that it may give grace to those who hear"* (Ephesians 4:29 NASB). Greek is the language in which this letter was originally written. The literal Greek word that is translated as "unwholesome word" in English is "putrid." Paul labels harmful speech as putrid. When my trash can outside gets dirty, we might say it smells bad, even terrible. But after sitting out in the hot, North Carolina, August sun for a week, filled with the remains of a poolside fish feast, it smells putrid. The smell can peel the paint off the car when the trash can is wheeled past! We call that smell putrid. The apostle Paul says that any type of communication that tears down is classified as putrid. The verse instructs us not to let anything of that nature come out of our mouths. Why? Because words are so powerful and the wrong kind can kill or irreparably damage a relationship. Solomon wrote in the Book of Proverbs that, *"Death and life are in the power of the tongue"* (Proverbs 18:21 NKJV). With the tongue we can kill relationships by damaging people. How many times have we said something we

> The apostle Paul says that any type of communication that tears down is classified as putrid.

immediately regretted? Even as the words are leaving our lips, regret has taken root in our hearts and we wish we could reel them back in and rephrase or eliminate them altogether. But the look on the face of the one to whom we have spoken tells us that it is too late, and our words have already done their damage. In that moment, the idea that "words will never hurt me" is overshadowed by the reality that death is sometimes in the power of the tongue. Those who are on the receiving end of putrid communication would gladly take a rock or two in place of the pain that words can bring.

Damaging words not only hurt those to whom they are directed, but the consequences they produce extend to a wider sphere. Paul identifies that sphere as "those who hear." When a co-worker is vilified in front of the office staff, all who are in range of the tirade are defiled. Who knows what affect the scene will have on those who are involved, and how the relationships of all the parties will be impacted? Those overhearing may lose respect for one or both. They may even avoid contact with the one inflicting the verbal abuse, fearful of a similar result from interaction with him in the future. Certainly, the real losers in open verbal battles in the home are not the parents who are involved in the fight, but the children who are standing by, listening to the ones they love the most, tearing each other down. In many cases, the winner of these conflicts is often the loser in the sight of the sons and daughters, since the one most hurt draws out the sympathy of the children. Sometimes "those who hear" are not the ones in direct hearing when painful words were spoken. Often, people repeat damaging words that have been spoken to them, adding their own interpretive twist for those with whom they share. Who knows what affect down the line this will have on the one listening? Many times this results in a subtle undermining of the relationship of the hearer with the one who originally spoke. The unfortunate thing is that the one now talked about doesn't have the privilege of adding their perspective. Often they don't even know they are being discussed, nor are they aware of the opinions being formed of them by others. Had they anticipated such, they might have exercised restraint before letting the painful words leave their lips.

Words can bring life

Not only can words produce death by killing relationships and damaging people, but words can also produce life. In commanding the reader to prohibit putrid communication from proceeding out of our mouths, Paul exhorts with another idea. Speaking the kinds of things that edify or build up others imparts grace to all who hear. Most people find it easy to tear others down. It is human nature to be critical when dealing with others. Out of pride and insecurity, we instinctively measure others by the opinion we hold of ourselves. We ignore the strengths we see in them, especially those that highlight our personal weaknesses, and we major on the faults of others, especially those that fall into the areas in which we normally shine. But, with a little effort and an exercise of humility, we can learn the art of affirmation. Right now, take stock of yourself. Are you affirming in your relationships? Do people look forward to being with you, because they always leave your company feeling built up? It is just as easy to build others up as it is to tear them down, and it is many times more rewarding! Words can produce life just as readily as they produce death. Indeed, Solomon includes both in the same saying: *"Death and life are in the power of the tongue"* (Proverbs 18:21, NKJV). Acknowledging the tongue as a powerful tool, Solomon points out that its power is found in its ability to produce *both life and death.*

> With a little effort and an exercise of humility, we can learn the art of affirmation.

The list of ways in which words can build up is endless. Paul used the phrase, *"according to the need of the moment"*. Wherever there is a need, there is an opportunity to build others up through our interaction with them. We must learn to use the needs of those around us as signposts, pointing to occasions for edification. When a co-worker is under obvious stress about a project, encouraging him by reminding him of past successes is a great way to build him up. When your spouse is frustrated by the pressures of having more month at the end of the money, a positive word can go a long way. Telling a struggling employee that you admire the quality of his or her work is a great way to break them out of a creative slump. Sometimes effective communication requires that words not be spoken. Sitting beside a friend in a hospital waiting room, holding her hand, and keeping her coffee cup filled, communicates support more than a thousand words could ever convey.

When we build up the people around us with our words and actions, those to whom we communicate are not the only winners. Remember the sphere defined as "those who hear" from Ephesians 4:29? Those who are indirect recipients of edification are built up as well. Think of the times you have read an inspiring story or heard a great testimony. All those down the line are built up as your spouse tells the tale of the wonderful thing you said to them. Employees eagerly spread the compliment paid to them by the boss. Children prosper in an environment where parents routinely value each other with their words.

> We must learn to use the needs of those around us as signposts, pointing to occasions for edification.

Not only do others down the line benefit, but, as with damaging words, affirming words have a marvelous "boomerang effect." What do employees think of a boss who admires their work and passes out compliments accordingly? What do children think of a father who makes it clear that he loves their mother? Increased loyalty is the prize parents enjoy from their children, when their sons and daughters routinely recognize their parents as their greatest cheerleaders. Your words have the power to build, and everyone loves to be built up. Edifying words actually give grace to those who hear them, thus producing life. That which tears down naturally repels people, but they are irresistibly drawn to that which gives life. Mastering the art of affirmation is the greatest gift you could give yourself. When you are affirming of others, you cannot escape the impact on your own reputation. Simply put, you become more attractive to people.

Communication is the lifeline of every relationship, but the quality of what passes through that lifeline determines the health of those relationships. "Bad air" can slowly kill a diver. Negative and hurtful words destroy people. The right gasses, carefully mixed and monitored, can enable a diver to work beneath the surface for hours. Healthy communication can keep a flow of life in our interaction with others, producing strong and lasting relationships. The Bible includes a long list of the kinds of communication that kill. Only a few are mentioned below:

angry words	lying (exaggeration)
hasty words	flattery
rash words	gossip
harsh words	slander
condemning words	complaining
unkind words	cursing
bitter words	quarreling
mocking words	scoffing
foolish words	comparison
critical words	backbiting

It is hard to read the list without finding something we have done wrong, perhaps even habitually. Remember, every need provides an opportunity for building up, even the needs we create with our own damaging words! Again, it is time to take stock. Read the list again and identify those relationships in which you have employed harmful modes of communication. As hard as it may seem, purpose now to go to each of those people and seek their forgiveness. Humble yourself and take responsibility for the pain you have caused them. Be very careful what you promise. When we are just beginning to build a new habit, failure is certain, especially in matters pertaining to the tongue. Telling your spouse that you will never criticize them again is probably making a promise you cannot keep. Telling them that you are working on this area of your life is probably a better and more realistic approach.

Building successful relationships is the result of winning and keeping the hearts of others. Hearts are won and kept as we apply the six principles listed in the previous chapters in this book. But these principles are only as efficient as our channels of communication are effective. Don't ever forget—"bad air" kills, but affirmation produces life!

Questions for your relational journey

1. "Sticks and stones can break my bones but words will never hurt me." True or false? Illustrate your answer with examples from your own life.

2. Why is it that without communication relationships die?

3. There are many types of communication, not all of which are positive. Reread the list of negative and destructive forms of communication. Do you ever employ any of these in your relationships? Which areas in your life need the most work?

4. What kind of words bring life to the hearer? What forms of positive communication are most likely to build you up?

5. In which of your relationships do you most need to develop the art of affirmation? Make a list right now of ways you can build that person up.

chapter 9

"Neither Magic Nor Manipulation"

We live today in what I call a "microwave society." Everywhere you go, people want it now and they want it hot. But, true lasting relationships don't come from a mix we can toss into a bowl and heat up in the microwave. They take effort and are slowly baked over time. Often people come for counsel when a relationship turns "south." Waiting too late and hoping for a quick fix, they come seeking a magic formula that can make everything right. Some take the advice they receive and begin to work their way out of the relationship hole they have dug for themselves. Daily applying the principles outlined in this book, they seek to win back the heart they see slipping away. Others leave disheartened. They had hoped to find the one prayer or the one new idea that would do the trick. Let me make it clear, these ideas are not magic formulas.

The myth of the magical shortcut

Magic is big today, driven by a society seeking instant answers to problems caused by more complicated factors. These principles contain no magical power, no power of enchantment to make people love you. These ideas create the environment where hearts can be won and facilitate the process by which they can be kept. Magic, by definition, is an attempt to override the will of others by applying a set of "laws" that contain unseen powers. By applying these "laws," we can force people to do things, feel things, or become things against their will. I fear some will take these powerful truths and seek to use them in the wrong way.

While it is true, as we have already said, that no one is safe from the potential theft of their heart by another, it is also true that no one's heart is "stolen" against their will. Actually, hearts are won step-by-step or piece-by-piece. As we serve someone or spend time with someone, their heart opens to us a little more. Even if at first we weren't on their favorite person list, by encouraging them or listening to their life story, we are putting ourselves in a position to work our way into their hearts. Day by day, the recipient of our effort has the opportunity to change their mind about us, and more importantly, change the status of their heart toward us.

> While it is true, as we have already said, that no one is safe from the potential theft of their heart by another, it is also true that no one's heart is "stolen" against their will.

Faith, availability, interest, and the other ideas contained in this book are not parts of a potion that can be mixed and sprinkled on the co-worker in the cubicle next to us, to make them fall in love with us. In the end, the co-worker will have to cooperate with the process and make choices along the way. When they feel their heart "going out," they must choose to let the process continue along its natural course unhindered, or decide to cut off the relationship where it stands, halting any further progress. Perhaps they are married and begin to recognize that all this time spent with a co-worker is detrimental to the future of their relationship

> Manipulation has "self" at the center, and it sees people as pawns to provide the benefits of life for personal consumption.

with their spouse. Thank God these truths are not part of a magic formula that can override our human will, and thereby force us into something we do not want.

We are dealing with people, and we have already made clear the fact that every relationship includes risk and the potential for pain since our hearts are involved. What I can guarantee is that these applications will put you in the best position to win and keep the hearts of others.

Manipulation

Webster's dictionary defines manipulation as "influencing or attempting to influence the behavior or emotions of others for one's own benefit." Manipulation has "self" at the center, and it sees people as pawns to provide the benefits of life for personal consumption. It is a perversion of everything I have tried to put forward in this book.

I know that these truths are open to misuse in the hands of unscrupulous people bent on having their own way. Selfish, self-centered people will use whatever means necessary to accomplish their goals and obtain what they desire. I also know that most people are capable of seeing through the ruse, discerning the true motives of their pursuer. Truths applied from motives drenched in falsehood will not produce positive lasting results. Manipulation always destroys!

Over the years I have seen manipulation take various forms. Fred was convinced that Andrea was the one for him, so he pursued her with a vengeance. If he were to read this book today, he might assume that he had done everything right but never received his prize. In fact, she ran from him with everything she had. He continued to chase her, and in so doing, he chased her right into the arms of another man, with whom she fell in love and eventually married.

Pushing others away

Fred had two problems that stripped the power right out of the truths he applied, actually causing them to have a reverse effect. First, his motive was self-centered. His care for Andrea was not truly driven out of a desire for what best benefited her. He was seeking a wife for himself. In the end, his actions were all about Fred and what was good for him. Second, he pushed. When you push people, you drive them away. You never push someone *toward* yourself. That attitude betrays the true motive of the heart. The person that pushes is a person who is dominated by his or her own agenda. The moment they begin to push, they force that agenda on the wills of those with whom they are dealing, and that repulses people. Make it clear in your mind, that when you push, you push people away.

When a father decides that, after years of totally neglecting his teenager, they are now going to be best buddies and weekly golfing partners, he is running the risk of turning his son away. When a young man sets his sights on a young lady and follows her everywhere she goes, she ends up feeling stalked rather than wooed. When you attempt to spend every waking moment with the new friend in the dorm room across the hall, they can feel smothered and not befriended. It won't be long before they will be avoiding you altogether.

The "poor me" approach

Sometimes in attempting to manipulate those they love, people head in the opposite direction. Rather than pushing, they take the "poor me" approach. Mistaking sympathy for love, they cast themselves in the role of the broken one, hoping the emotion they draw out of people will somehow mutate into something upon which they can build.

In the last chapter, I mentioned how Harold had run off his wife with his mouth. If that had been all that happened, perhaps we could have reasoned with Cindy to return. Against all advice, Harold first pursued Cindy by pushing his way back into her life: "You can't do this. We have been married 20 years, and I won't stand for it." He quickly learned that this was a dead end road, but then he tried another approach with increasingly disastrous results—he groveled. He quit eating well and made sure she noticed. He sent flowers, something he hadn't done in years, with notes begging her to come home. He visited her at work, and with pleading eyes, spoke of the love he held for her in his heart. This form of manipulation never works for three reasons.

First, to grovel you must totally set aside all measure of self-respect. People have no respect for those who do not respect themselves. Rarely, when we are in this mode do we really take a good look at ourselves. We walk around with a look of desperation on our face. Groveling only makes you appear pitiful, and the only emotion elicited through that method is pity—a far cry from the love we crave.

Second, groveling is another form of pushing! It seeks to fulfill its own desire by forcing the departed heart to come home. The only difference is the method, but the motive is the same. Self is at the center, and it does whatever it thinks is necessary to make the loved one comply.

Third, one of the main points of this book, is that hearts are *kept* the same way they are *won*. And, hearts are won back the same way they were won in the first place. Do you suppose Harold begged Cindy, with desperation in his voice, the first time he asked her out? Did he grovel outside her apartment, or interrupt her every day at work to get her to notice him? No way! He instinctively applied several of the seven principles taught in this book, and he won her heart. Now that her heart has strayed away, he will need to revisit the methods he used at first, with even greater patience, giving her all the space she needs to allow for the rekindling of affection.

> Groveling only makes you appear pitiful, and the only emotion elicited through that method is pity—a far cry from the love we crave.

Manipulation through changing roles

Another form of manipulation manifests itself in people stepping outside the normal parameters of their position to pursue a relationship. At first glance this seems noble, but a deeper look reveals manipulation at work. A college professor, friendless and alone, sets aside his place of esteem to try "hanging out with the guys." Unsure how to handle his suggestion, and intimidated by his authority, the students invite the scholar out for a night on the town. By evening's end, the students have lost all respect for the professor and see him as weak and pitiful. Parents, reaching for the heart of a child they see slipping away, sometimes depart from their role as parent and take on the role of friend. But "learning the lingo" and "donning the duds" won't erase twenty years of age separation and cultural orientation.

> Lowering yourself from parent to the position of friend will not win the respect of your child.

Besides, children have tons of friends, but only two parents. Lowering yourself from parent to the position of friend will not win the respect of your child. In fact, it will have the opposite effect. What will your son say to his friends when asked, "Hey, dude, what's up with your dad? What trip is he on?" Now you add embarrassment to the list of indictments your son has against you.

Why is this manipulation? Because it seeks to bring people back into a relationship we once enjoyed with them, without first asking ourselves the tough questions concerning what we may have done to damage that relationship in the first place. Once again, self is at the center. All seven areas talked about in this book set the other person at the center. Our focus is on loving them, having faith for them, serving them, and being available to them—because we enjoy them, not because we want them to enjoy us. If our focus is on getting back what we once had for our own benefit, we betray ourselves and reveal our true heart. In the end, we make matters worse, not better.

Perhaps our approach should be to, first, humble ourselves and take a look at where we have allowed for the downward spiral of the relationship. Which of the seven applications have we habitually neglected? In some cases, we might find out that we have been, for the most part, faithful, and that the other party is the one who has strayed. Perhaps someone has stolen the heart of the one we love. Whatever the case, let's begin with ourselves, attempting to detect what adjustment we might need to make. Second, take inventory of the needs of your loved one. Create a plan to apply the principles listed here to meet those needs. Make your loved one the focus. They are the one you are seeking to benefit. Let any benefit that comes to you be a bonus. Your main reward is in seeking the highest good of your loved one. Third, be patient, and don't be too quick to assess the results of what you are doing. Unfortunately, things sometimes get worse before they get better. If a spouse, for instance, has allowed their heart to go out to a co-worker, your overtures of affection may increase the guilt they feel. Normally, the first stage of that conviction demonstrates itself with increased irritation. Often, the convicted party will seek to limit contact with the one prompting those guilty feelings. Be patient and increase creativity. What you are doing is having the desired effect.

Trying to override the will of another to get what you want is always wrong, and there are no short cuts in building strong relationships. The most valuable things in life take time to cultivate. And remember, all forms of manipulation,

Let any benefit that comes to you be a bonus. Your main reward is in seeking the highest good of your loved one.

including pushing, groveling, and stepping out of our place, will always produce negative results. I wanted to be very clear on the dangers of looking for magical short cuts and utilizing manipulative methods.

Questions for your relational journey

1. These seven applications are not magical formulas. They simply place one in a position to win or keep the hearts of others. Go over the seven applications again and discuss how each works to attract others to yourself. Now discuss how others may resist the process!

2. How could one use these principles from a wrong motive? Manipulation (using these principles for selfish gain) will not produce positive results in the long run. Why not?

3. How does trying to push someone into a relationship actually have a reverse affect?

4. Why is groveling ineffective in restoring a damaged relationship?

chapter 10

"Of Dogwoods and Dogfights"

No one ever cuts down a dogwood tree, and yet there I was, cutting down the second one in as many months. And this one was right there in the middle of my front yard. Not only did I feel like a botanical failure, but I was embarrassed. (My father doesn't have a green thumb but a whole green forearm. He can get stuff to grow in concrete. And my mother knows the name of every plant in the book!) So, as I cut the formerly beautiful tree into pieces for curbside pick-up, I eyed the largest, most spectacular of the remaining dogwoods in my yard. The branch in the middle had completely lost its leaves and was slowly drying up. I was losing another one! Something had to be done.

I called in an expert who immediately diagnosed the problem. These trees weren't struck by lightning, and they hadn't been hit by a car. They were being eaten by a disease. I was off the hook, or so I thought! "I am not responsible for this. Some tree disease got them—just bad luck." Wrong! My expert squatted down by the trunk of the remaining trees and showed me the problem. As it turns out, every time I cut the grass in my zeal to manicure the lawn as neatly as possible, I had cut too closely to the trees. The constant rubbing over the four years we had lived in the house, had damaged the protective bark around the base of the tree, allowing access to destructive diseases. Without realizing it, I was killing my own trees with my own hands. The trees ultimately died due to the effects of long-term damage.

Relational neglect

Most relationships that die end the same way. Someone has neglected to do regular maintenance on them and allowed for the relationship to slowly slide downhill. Most storms that spring up overnight, even the severe ones, can be weathered with little damage. Going through a storm or two actually makes plants stronger. In the time we resided in this particular house, prior to losing the trees, we had lived through two devastating hurricanes, and the dogwoods faired quite nicely. It wasn't the short-term crises that did the trees in, but long-term abuse. The same is true of relationships. Crises often pull us together instead of tearing us apart, even though, in the midst of the storm, we wonder if we will make it. In the end, when the clouds of crisis dissipate, and we emerge into the light of day, we find ourselves working side by side to make things better again. Families, during times of financial struggle, often fear that the pressure will tear them apart and destroy their children. In the end, however, the pressure only serves to drive them closer together.

On our family farm in Michigan stands an old walnut tree that has been struck more than once by lightning. Fortunately, that tree has survived, but there are times when a blow as severe as lightening can completely destroy a tree. Likewise, sometimes the blow of infidelity can completely wipe-out a marriage. If the husband, after years of hidden affairs, is suddenly discovered, the blow may be too much, depending on the health of the marriage. But it isn't usually the one strike of lightening that splits a relationship apart. Long-term damage allows for disease to enter the relationship, weakening it from within. Then when the storm clouds gather, and lightening strikes, the relationship does not have the strength to go on.

The point is simple—relationships are not usually lost due to short-term crisis. They erode over time. Every week, I contributed to the demise of my dogwoods, never realizing what I was doing. These seven principles we have been talking about are not optional in building lasting relationships. These are the things that cause relationships to develop in the first place, and these are the things that enable them to last. We don't have to become experts in botany, but we should aspire to become experts in building strong relationships, because these are the most important things in life.

> Relationships are not usually lost due to short-term crisis.

Sowing seeds and nurturing

But there is good news in this lesson. Those trees that enjoy long-term maintenance are the ones that live the longest and produce the most beautiful blossoms. The dogwoods that grow wild in the woods are plentiful, but they are never as beautiful as the ones growing in the yards of thoughtful owners who spray, fertilize and manicure them in the early years. A relationship that has been the recipient of long-term care is strong and able to weather storms with ease. Those with good root systems, built over the years, actually benefit from storms that harm or destroy others. Here is the point—it is much harder to lose a relationship that is healthy than one that is weak. The more you take care of it, the harder it is for it to die. The more you apply these seven truths, the greater the hold you have on the hearts of the ones you love. A wife whose needs are continually met by her loving husband is not a likely candidate for the theft of her heart by a better-looking male co-worker. In fact, any attempt at all to steal her heart will probably serve to drive her closer to her husband!

Sowing the right kind of seeds in the fertile ground of youth is the best way to build lifelong relationships with your children. But, as children grow, the relationship must grow with them. We can't expect the fertilizer we put into the ground two years ago to still produce the desired effect. We need a fresh application of the stuff to keep the garden growing. It pains me to hear adult children talk about their parents like they are less then former acquaintances. Someone stopped sowing the right kind of seeds, and they relied on old fertilizer to make what little they had planted grow. Long-term application of these seven truths makes for long-term health in our relationships.

But what if we have neglected to do the right things for some time? What should we do? Is it too late? Should we give up? Before I answer this, let me tell you two stories.

The history of O'Hare

I had flown through O'Hare airport in Chicago too many times to count, but I never gave another thought about its name or how it came to be called O'Hare. But, the story of Butch

O'Hare is one of the most inspiring I have ever heard. Navy Lt. Commander Edward Henry (Butch) O'Hare was a World War II hero. After growing up in Chicago's south side, Butch O'Hare was not one to shrink back from a fight. Having attended the US Naval Academy, Butch was assigned to the Pacific fleet. A Navy pilot, Butch flew one of the many Grumman F4F fighters assigned to the *USS Lexington*.

On February 20, 1942, while the rest of the squadron was parked on board the carrier, Butch's fighter was the only US plane in the air as the fleet sailed near the Gilbert Islands. While the rest of the fighters fueled and reloaded on the carrier's massive deck, Butch spotted a squadron of nine Japanese bombers heading directly for the American fleet, just four brief minutes away.

Without hesitation Butch thrust himself into harms way in an effort to save the fleet from sure destruction. Alone in the sky, Butch propelled his single engine Hellcat directly into the path of the bombers. The film records, in the wing-mounted camera, verify reports that Butch flew his plane within twenty yards of some aircraft. He was close enough to see the horror on the face of the Japanese pilots, as he unloaded his .50-caliber machine guns into their bomber's hull. The enemy squadron was in disarray, as the lone fighter pilot did everything he could do to disrupt their course and save the fleet. In pass after pass, Butch braved the hail of enemy fire, as he swooped in dangerously close to the Japanese planes. Out-numbered and out-gunned, Butch continued his assault without regard to personal safety. First one bomber, then another burst into flames, as they dropped into the sea below. Finally, the bombers attempted to withdraw, having lost five of their original nine to Butch's relentless heroics. But by now, more American fighters had entered the fray, destroying three additional planes. The only bomber to escape was damaged in a shootout with O'Hare and is believed to have crashed in the sea somewhere in the Pacific.

For his heroism, Butch O'Hare was awarded the Congressional Medal of Honor and became the first Navy Ace of World War II. President Franklin D. Roosevelt said of O'Hare that his was, "One of the most daring, if not the most daring, single action in the history of combat aviation." On November 26, 1943, while flying another combat mission, Butch was shot down and lost at sea. In 1949, 200,000 people turned out to witness the renaming of Chicago's Orchard Depot to O'Hare International Airport, after one of the city's favorite sons. What this has to do with building successful relationships will become clear after one more important story.

The redemption of a crooked lawyer

Easy Eddie, as he was called, was a very good lawyer. His reputation was less than honorable, since his employer and business partner was none other than Alphonse (Al) Capone, perhaps America's best known and most feared criminal.

In his early days, Eddie made his money in dog racing. Eddie had swindled the wife of a former business partner out of the rights to the patent for the mechanical rabbit—the centerpiece of the dog racing enterprise. The only people really investing in dog racing at the time were Mob figures, which brought Eddie into contact with Capone. Soon Eddie and Al opened a string of dog tracks in various parts of the country. After dog racing was declared illegal, the two converted the tracks to horse racing establishments. Eventually, Eddie was in charge of the entire operation.

Not only did Easy Eddie take care of the racing business, but he acted as Capone's chief legal counsel. In this capacity he dealt with the murder, prostitution, and racketeering arrests of those in Capone's organization. In one stretch of 15 months, Eddie orchestrated the dismissal of gambling charges against 12,000+ defendants! He was good at what he did, and he was heavily rewarded for his efforts. Capone provided him with everything he could ever want. Eddie had servants, cars, and anything money could buy. His house was so large, it occupied one entire city block. Capone had to watch out for Easy Eddie, since the attorney knew everything about everyone in his crime syndicate. Eddie was the picture of the corrupt lawyer.

But in stark contrast to his corruption, Eddie was also a doting father, and he wanted the very best for his son. It was widely known in his circles that Eddie would do anything to secure a better future for his son. He put him in the best schools and tried to protect him from the life he was living. He would spare no expense to accomplish this goal. Nearing graduation from high school, Eddie's son made it clear that his dream was to attend an armed services academy. No amount of money could ever provide that type of education—a Congressional appointment was required, and there was no way he could ever buy that. His son's dreams would have to go unfulfilled.

It was then that Eddie recognized his error. He had placed his focus on providing financially and had neglected to provide his son with the two things he needed most—a good name and a reputation to go with it. Somehow, he needed to do something to redeem the wasted years. Eddie contacted Federal prosecutors through a newspaperman named John Rogers. In a short time, the prosecutors made a deal with a congressman to grant an appointment to Eddie's son in exchange for the lawyer's testimony against Capone. Having worked with Capone for years, Eddie knew exactly what this would mean. In an act of heroism, Easy Eddie bought redemption for his name and his son with the price of his life. After receiving an 11 year sentence, Capone was in a rage. On November 8, 1939, Eddie was gunned down while driving in his black Lincoln coupe. Twenty-seven months later, Butch O'Hare followed in the steps of his father's heroism, plowing his fighter into the fray over the Gilbert Islands, saving the *USS Lexington*, and protecting the US fleet. Yes, Butch O'Hare was Easy Eddie's son!

> In giving our lives away, we get more than our lives in return; we get the hearts of those to whom we give our lives as well.

So, what if we have neglected to do the right things for some time? What should we do? Is it too late? Should we give up? I doubt anyone reading this book is as notorious and unscrupulous as Easy Eddie. If he could mend his ways and set things right, so can you. We can learn two very important lessons from him. "But it cost him his life," one might retort. No doubt it will cost us as well. Eddie paid by giving his life and so must we. We may not have to pay unto death, but giving ourselves to others is what is required. As we give our time, our attention, our love, our service, we are giving our lives away. That is the first lesson. In giving our lives away, we get more than our lives in return; we get the hearts of those to whom we give our lives as well. The second lesson is simply this – no matter how much time we have wasted, it is never too late to begin. In fact, start now to sow into the relationships that surround your life. As we express faith, give unconditional love, put others first, are there when they need us, give them respect, invest our time in them, and keep the lifeline of communication open, we will continually win the hearts of those we love!

Questions for your relational journey

1. Most relationships that fail do so over time. Like trees, long-term damage allows disease to enter the relationship, weakening it from within. How, in your experience, have you seen this to be true?

2. By the same token, relationships that have enjoyed regular maintenance (healthy doses of the seven principles mentioned here) are able to weather the storms of life. Share a story from your own life that illustrates this point.

3. When is the right time to begin rebuilding a damaged relationship?

4. When is it too late? Can broken relationships be mended? Do you know of any that have been restored? If so, share the story to amplify your answer.

"One Profound Truth, Seven Applications"

Everyone wants their relationships to succeed. No one gets up in the morning hoping their relationships will fail. Instead, we all dream of that story-book marriage for ourselves and our children. We desire to be more effective in our business relationships. We want our friendships to grow and desire to be close to our children forever. The trouble is, that most people have no clue as to how to go about making this happen. They walk out into life with a hope and a prayer, letting the chips fall as they may; they have no idea how to intentionally build strong, lasting relationships. But not you. You know better.

You know that the heart is the centerpiece of life. It is that part of a human that governs everything. And whoever has the heart, has the life! Your spouse is in love with whoever has their heart. Your friends desire to spend time with whoever has their hearts. Your children will follow whoever has their hearts. Your clients are drawn to whoever has their hearts. The key to building the successful relationships of which we dream is winning and keeping the hearts of others.

Seven key principles are central to the application of this profound truth to life. Master these, and you have mastered the art of winning and keeping hearts.

1. **Love**—Loving others without condition
2. **Faith**—Believing more for someone than they do for themselves
3. **Interest**—Placing value on what is important to others
4. **Availability**—Making room for others in crisis and in life
5. **Respect**—Establishing a person's worth
6. **Time**—The key to unlocking a heart
7. **Communication**—The lifeline to every relationship

Always remember, the most important things in life are the relationships that give life meaning. Money is nice, but it can never provide true happiness. That only comes as a by-product of healthy relationships. Seek to become an expert at unconditionally loving those in your life. Look for ways to express faith in the lives of those you love. Develop the skill of being interested in people, by being interested in the things that matter most to them. Make people a priority by being there when they need you. Everyone craves respect, so find ways to give it to them. Remember that your time is your life, and investing that time in people is key to opening their hearts. Never let the lifeline of communication become choked off—without it, no relationship can survive.

As the old saying goes, "Today is the first day of the rest of your life." Make today count. Start now to develop new habits that will yield the richest of dividends in the areas that matter most—your relationships!

Resources

Larry Jackson and Michael Fletcher

Beyond Reconciliation

Establishing Long-Lasting, Life-Giving Relationships Across Racial Boundaries

By Michael Fletcher and Larry Jackson
65 pages, $5.95

With God using so many leaders to bring the message of racial reconciliation across our country, and with so many individuals coming forward at conferences to become "reconciled," why are so few people experiencing a real covenant relationship with a brother or sister of a different cultural background? Why are so few churches becoming truly multiethnic? And why are so few cities being impacted to the degree that the press has no race riot or protest to report after a major hate crime is committed? What we must realize is that reconciliation messages and meetings, while important, are only the starting point. In sharing their own story of an extraordinary covenant friendship, Larry Jackson and Michael Fletcher reveal many important principles for fostering true racial unity.

To order a copy visit: **www.advancethekingdom.com** or call 910-867-9151

Also available from Michael Fletcher

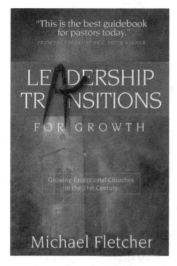

Leadership Transitions for Growth

Growing Exceptional Churches in the 21st Century

127 pages, $10.95

Every growing church will eventually hit different barriers, causing increased tension among leadership as well as the congregation. It can stop the growth of the church in its tracks. When one of these barriers arises, the church will need to make internal transitions to move forward and see continued growth. In this practical book, Michael Fletcher skillfully defines the difference from one stage of a church's life to the next, and gives clear, insightful instruction on implementing key leadership transitions to bring new life and growth to any church.

"This book Is the best guidebook for pastors today"
From the Forward by C. Peter Wagner

To order a copy visit: **www.advancethekingdom.com** or call 910-867-9151

Audio Teachings

Becoming the Person You Were Destined to Be (6 tapes or CDs) $30.00

Beyond Surviving (5 tapes or CDs)... $25.00

Bless and Curse Not (5 tapes or CDs)... $25.00

Building Successful Families in Stressful Times (5 tapes or CDs) $25.00

The Discovery Series (4 tapes or CDs)... $20.00

Freedom Training (with David Schmaltz. 8 tapes or CDs).............. $30.00

The Glory Returns (2 tapes or CDs)... $10.00

How to Pray In Everything You Need (5 tapes or CDs) $25.00

The Key to Everything (4 tapes or CDs) $20.00

The Keys of the Kingdom (8 tapes or CDs) $30.00

The King and His Kingdom (7 tapes or CDs)................................. $30.00

Living in the Promised Land (7 tapes or CDs) $30.00

Prayer According to Jesus (3 tapes or CDs) $15.00

Reaching for the Prize (4 tapes or CDs) $20.00

Rearing a Godly Generation (5 tapes or CDs + study guide) $30.00

Six Laws that Govern the Use of the Tongue (8 tapes or CDs) $30.00

Unlocking the Power of Prayer (6 tapes or CDs) $30.00

When the Spirit Speaks (5 tapes or CDs) $25.00

You Are Not the Weakest Link (8 tapes or CDs) $30.00

Experiencing Lasting Change (3 tapes or CDs) $15.00

Your Greatest Asset (2 tapes or CDs) $10.00

Video Teachings

Rearing a Godly Generation (2 VHS + study guide) $35.00

To order these resources or copies of *Building Successful Relationships* visit:
www.advancethekingdom.com or call 910-867-9151